iDentities

PAUL SELIGSON, LUIZ OTÁVIO BARROS
and ALASTAIR LANE

STUDENT'S BOOK
& WORKBOOK
COMBO EDITION

1B

Richmond

Language Map – Student's Book

		Speaking / Topic	Grammar	Vocabulary / Strategies	Writing
7	7.1	How important is music to you?		Success expressions; talking about changing tastes	
	7.2	What was your most recent disappointment?	Conjunctions to express purpose and reason: *(in order) to, so (that), as, since, because (of)*, and *due to*	Uses of *so*	
	7.3	What's the best movie you've seen?		Failure expressions; words that are nouns, verbs, or both	
	7.4	When was the last time you went to a museum?	Modifying nouns: *another, some other* and *the others*		
	7.5	Which musician do you listen to the most?			Writing a review: using adverbs effectively
8	8.1	Has fear ever held you back?		Expressing fears; physical symptoms of fear	
	8.2	Are you good at improvising?	Describing past ability: *could* and *was / were able to*		
	8.3	How much attention do you pay to the news?		Common verb + noun collocations	
	8.4	What prevents you from traveling more?	Expressing obligation, permission, and advice: *must / have (got) to, had better, be allowed to, be supposed to*, and *should / ought to*		
	8.5	Who do you usually turn to for advice?			A message of advice: using friendly comments for naturalness
	Review 4 *p.92*				
9	9.1	How much time do you spend on your own?	Word order for objects and phrasal verbs	Verbs and expressions for interacting with people	
	9.2	What behavior is rude in your culture?	Uses of *which* in non-restrictive clauses		
	9.3	What does your age group worry about the most?		Describing attitudes	
	9.4	Would you be a good detective?	Reduced relative clauses: active and passive		
	9.5	What do you spend the most money on?		Developing an argument (3)	A problem-solution essay: conjunctions to express purpose, to compare, to concede, and to express reason
10	10.1	How do you like to get around town?		Phrasal verbs; talking about unexpected events	
	10.2	What's your idea of a perfect vacation?	Negative questions; indirect questions: *Wh-* and *yes-no*	Forming nouns from phrasal verbs	
	10.3	Which foreign country would you most like to live in?		Words with literal and figurative meanings	
	10.4	Has your daily routine changed over time?	Talking about acquired habits: *be* and *get used to*		
	10.5	Which are your two favorite cities and why?			A travel report: using synonyms and figurative expressions in descriptions
	Review 5 *p.114*				

Language Map – Student's Book

	Speaking / Topic	Grammar	Vocabulary / Strategies	Writing
11 11.1	What recent news has caught your eye?		Words and expressions for talking about the news	
11.2	Have you ever laughed at the wrong moment?	Reporting what people say (1): reported statements and questions		
11.3	What was the last video you shared?		Expressions for emotional reactions	
11.4	What's your definition of gossip?	Reporting what people say (2): reporting patterns with the infinitive and base form	Expressions for gossiping	
11.5	Would you enjoy being world famous?			A letter of complaint: writing a formal email
12 12.1	How optimistic are you?		Expressing optimism and pessimism	
12.2	Will the world be better in 100 years?	Talking about the future (1): predictions with *going to*, *will*, future perfect and future continuous	Uses of *by*; other ways to make predictions	
12.3	What's the coldest place you've been to?		Expressions for discussing innovation	
12.4	What was the last excuse you made?	Talking about the future (2): expressing plans and intentions, decisions, and scheduled events; time clauses		
12.5	What will your life be like 10 years from now?		Expressions for degrees of certainty	An email to your future self: using adverbs for emphasis

Review 6 *p.136*

Grammar expansion *p.150*

Selected audio scripts *p.163*

Workbook contents

Phrasal verb list *p.119*

7 » How important is music to you?

1 Vocabulary: Success expressions

A In groups, share what you know about musicians 1–5. Remember any lines from their songs?

Yes! "Whenever, wherever, we're meant to be together ...". My favorite Shakira song!

B 7.1 Take the quiz. Listen to a radio show to check. Did you get any right?

RU an expert on pop-music trivia?
Try these four tricky questions to find out

1 Sam Smith **rose to fame** in 2012. What was his job before he became a **high-profile** celebrity?
- a a taxi driver
- b a bartender
- c a pet groomer

2 Jamaican Bob Marley (1945–1981) **is** generally **regarded as** the king of reggae. Which is true?
- a As a child, he could predict people's futures by reading their palms.
- b He only released three albums in his lifetime.
- c His biggest hit is *Don't worry, be happy.*

3 Adele's *21*, the best-selling album that **came out** in 2011, topped the charts for nearly six months. What does 21 refer to?
- a her lucky number
- b the number of songs on the CD
- c her age at the time

4 The first U.S. edition of the Rock in Rio music festival **took place** in 2015 and featured the singer behind the smash hits *Uptown funk* and *Grenade*. Was it ...?
- a Bruno Mars
- b Rihanna
- c Shakira

C 7.2 Match the highlighted words in **B** to their definitions. Listen to check.

1 rose to fame	a	☐	was officially released, became available
2 high-profile	b	☐	suddenly became very famous
3 is regarded as	c	☐	is considered
4 came out	d	☐	happened, occurred
5 took place	e	☐	prominent and well known

D **Make it personal** In groups, search online for *music trivia*. Write three questions to ask the class. Try to use some words from **C**. Who are the most popular artists?

OK, Calvin Harris is a high-profile Scottish DJ and singer. Which song did he produce? Was it a) ...

2 Listening

A 7.3 Listen to DJs Tim and Nina after their show. Why is Tim tired of his job?

☐ The pay's not good enough. ☐ His taste in music has changed.
☐ Music has changed.

B 7.3 Listen again. T (true) or F (false)? What do *you* think Tim should do?

1 Tim studied music in college.
2 Nina likes Coldplay.
3 Tim thinks pop songs have predictable melodies, but fine lyrics.
4 Nina seems to dislike the commercial side of pop music.
5 Their station probably has very young listeners.
6 Tim's considering applying for a non-radio job.

I think Tim should follow his heart and just quit.

Definitely, that's what I would do.

C **Make it personal** How have your tastes changed over the last decade?

1 7.4 **How to say it** Complete the sentences from the conversation. Listen to check.

Talking about changing tastes

	What they said	What they meant
Past	1 I used to be really ______ of (pop music).	I used to like pop music.
	2 I was really ______ (their music).	I really liked their music.
	3 I ______ tired of (playing the same songs).	I lost interest in playing the same songs
Present	4 I'm ______ hooked on (jazz).	I'm becoming fascinated by jazz.
	5 I can't ______ enough of (it).	I really, really like it.
	6 I've had ______ of (this job).	I'm sick of this job.

2 Choose three topics. Note down your tastes under "past" and "present."

clothes exercise food / drink movies music
radio / TV shows reading shopping sports

3 Share your ideas in groups. Use *How to say it* expressions. Many similarities?

I used to be really fond of *The Simpsons* when I was a kid. I wouldn't miss a single episode.

Common mistake

I'm really into / hooked on / tired of ~~read~~ reading gossip magazines.

3 Language in use

A 7.5 Listen to Liz sharing her experience with Josh. Choose the correct headline.

- [ ] MILEY CYRUS CANCELS CONCERT DUE TO SUDDEN ILLNESS
- [ ] DISAPPOINTING TICKET SALES FORCE CYRUS TO CANCEL KANSAS CONCERT
- [ ] CYRUS CONCERT CANCELED BECAUSE OF POWER OUTAGE

B 7.6 Read and predict the missing words. Listen to more of their conversation to check. Do you think Josh is a good listener?

KANSAS CITY, MO

Pop star Miley Cyrus has canceled Tuesday night's concert at the Sprint Center as she had a viral infection.

In a press release, the concert organizers said Cyrus was in a local __________ due to a severe allergic reaction to the __________ she was taking and would not be able to perform.

Ticket holders were told to proceed to the box office so that they could get a __________, but no further information was provided on whether the show would be rescheduled.

Cyrus tweeted a message in order to apologize to her __________: "Kansas, I promise I'm as heartbroken as you are. I wanted so badly 2 be there 2 night." ■

C 7.7 Read four extracts from what Liz said next and guess how 1) her story ends and 2) she feels about Miley now. Listen to check. Were you close?

Since I was on vacation, I thought I'd give her a second chance.

I left home early so I'd have plenty of time to get to the airport.

We nearly froze to death.

In the end, I downloaded the show just to have a taste of what I missed.

I think in the end Liz might not have ...

D **Make it personal** In pairs, which of these would(n't) you do in order to see and briefly meet your favorite artist(s)?

go into debt | miss school or work | sell something valuable
take an overnight bus | travel abroad | wait in line all day

I wouldn't mind waiting in line all day to meet Leonardo DiCaprio.

I might wait all day for an Alicia Keys concert, but it would depend on ...

E Read *Uses of so*. Then write 1–5 next to the examples in AS 7.7 on p.162.

Uses of *so*

So is in the top 50 most common words in spoken English. It is used to ...

1. keep the conversation going: ***So**, as I was saying, it was really cold and ...*
2. express a result: *It was a long journey, **so** I'm really exhausted.*
3. avoid repetition: *"Is Metallica playing in Peru this year?" "Yeah, I think **so**."*
4. intensify meaning: *Why do you have to be **so** difficult?*
5. express purpose: *Here's my number **so** you can text me.*

4 Grammar: Conjunctions to express purpose and reason

A Study the grammar box and check (✔) the correct rules.

Conjunctions: *(in order) to, so (that), as, since, because (of),* and *due to*

	Purpose	Reason
Neutral	Liz took a day off **to** see her idol. She bought front-row tickets **so** she could be near the stage.	**Because** / **Since** expectations were high, people were very frustrated. She canceled **because of** health reasons.
More formal	Cyrus tweeted **in order to** apologize. We went back **so that** we could get our money back.	**As** Cyrus had a viral infection, she had to take antibiotics. She was hospitalized **due to** an allergic reaction.

Use: a *In order to* + ☐ noun ☐ sentence ☐ verb
b *So (that), as, since,* and *because* + ☐ noun ☐ sentence ☐ verb
c *Because of* and *due to* + ☐ noun ☐ sentence ☐ verb

» Grammar expansion p.150

B Circle the correct answers. Then rewrite the text correctly using the incorrect choices.

CANCELED! THREE THAT (ALMOST) DIDN'T MAKE IT!

In 2009, MTV aired *The Osbournes Reloaded* [1][**so that / in order to**] they could repeat the success of the original reality show. However, it was canceled after only one episode [2][**because of / as**] it got terrible reviews.

Soccer fan Ric Wee made news in 2014 when he traveled 7,000 miles from Malaysia to the UK [3][**in order to / so that**] see his favorite team play live. But the game was postponed [4][**because / because of**] the bad weather.

Eighties British superstar Morrissey, who's a vegetarian, walked off stage a number of years ago in California [5][**since / because of**] the smell of barbecue coming from backstage. To his fans' relief, Morrissey went back [6][**to / so**] he could finish the show.

1 In 2009, MTV aired the Osbournes Reloaded in order to repeat the success of the original reality show.

C In pairs, complete headlines 1–5. Use *due to* and your own ideas. Then write one more headline.

1 **SMALL MEXICAN TOWN IN TOTAL PANIC ...**
Small Mexican town in total panic due to water shortage.
2 **ALL NEW YORK-BOUND FLIGHTS SUSPENDED ...**
3 **FINAL GAME MOVED TO (CHOOSE COUNTRY) ...**
4 **FAMOUS RESTAURANT CHAIN (CHOOSE ONE) CLOSES DOWN ...**
5 **MEGA-LOTTERY WINNER FAILS TO COLLECT PRIZE ...**

Common mistakes

The show was postponed because of / due to ~~it was raining heavily~~ *heavy rain*.

D Make it personal In groups, share your stories about events that were canceled, postponed, or that you missed. Use 1–5 to help you. Any happy endings?

1 Remember a(n) show / game / party / date / interview / trip ...
2 What happened exactly and why?
3 Whose fault was it?
4 How did you feel?
5 What happened in the end?

I missed my sister's wedding last year because of a power outage in my neighborhood.

Oh, no! What happened?

I got stuck in the elevator. And they couldn't get me out in time!

5 Reading

A Read paragraph 1 of the article. What do you think *flop* means?

B 7.8 Read and choose the best headings for paragraphs 2–4. There is an extra one. Listen to check.

Risk-taking	Reviews	The cost	Timing

Top of the Flops

– when the best made plans go wrong

1 In 2014, to promote the release of the iPhone 6, U2 made their new album available as a free download to iTunes users worldwide. In theory, a match made in heaven. But thousands of music fans resented the album being added to their libraries! In the end, what looked like a brilliant marketing strategy backfired and became one of the decade's biggest flops. But why? After all, how can anyone say no to a present? This episode shows just how hard it is to predict when something will make millions or flop embarrassingly and go nowhere. Here are three factors that we wrongly assume determine what's hot and what's not.

2 ________________: 2014's *Legends of Oz: Dorothy's Return* had a lot going for it. Loosely based on the *Wizard of Oz* story, it had tons of promotion and featured famous voices such as Lea Michele's, from *Glee*. Yet the movie made only $19 million worldwide – 27% of the production cost. Most people blame it on the critics. But if that's the case, how could a movie like *Teenage Mutant Ninja Turtles*, which critics disliked just as much, make nearly 200 million dollars in the same year?

3 ________________: Unless you were hiding in a cave in the late 2000s, there was no escaping the first *Twilight* movie, a smash hit despite the mixed reviews. Why did it become so massive? Possibly because it hit the screens just four months after the final *Twilight* novel, a cultural phenomenon. But then surely the same formula should have worked for *Joey*, released a few months after the wildly popular *Friends* finale in 2004. Yet *Joey* never caught on and was canceled due to poor ratings. So what did *Friends* have that *Joey* lacked? Maybe the chemistry between the characters, but it's hard to tell.

4 ________________: In the competitive New York theater scene, investors often base their musicals on proven hits. Take *Rocky the Musical*. Based on Sylvester Stallone's Oscar-winning movie, the show couldn't go wrong. It was far from a work of art, but it had an impressive production, masculine appeal, and pleasant songs. But, for whatever reason, *Rocky* failed to impress the public and didn't live up to expectations, running for six months only. Why did it never match the success of *Lion King*?

5 The truth is that no one really knows. Sometimes things just don't work as planned. Even with the most important ingredients in place, there is always an element of luck. C'est la vie!

C Re-read. T (true) or F (false)? Underline all the evidence.

1 iTunes users' reaction didn't come as a surprise.
2 *Legends of Oz* had a lot of potential.
3 The *Twilight* movies were extremely popular in the 2000s.
4 Musicals based on movies tend to be financially risky.
5 Broadway shows are never aimed at men.

D 7.9 Read *Noun, verb, or both?* In which two pairs of underlined words in the article does the meaning change? Listen to check.

Noun, verb, or both?

Nouns and verbs usually have the same meaning: *I sometimes* ***shop*** *(v) for rare CDs in a small record* ***shop*** *(n).*
But sometimes the meaning changes: *I'll be very upset if somebody's phone* ***rings*** *(v) during* ***Lord of the Rings*** *(n).*

Same	answer, cause, delay, damage, email, fight, guess, help, need, offer, practice, promise, rain, request, search, support, tweet, vote
Different	book, rock, show, trip

6 Vocabulary: Failure expressions

A Rewrite 1–5, substituting the bold words with the highlighted words in the article in 5B.

1 I had high hopes for the third season of *House of Cards*, but it **didn't** really **meet** my expectations.
I had high hopes for the third season of House of Cards, but it didn't live up to expectations.

2 The latest Stephen King novel **didn't manage to** generate any interest. Nobody talked about it.

3 I'll never understand why the latest Maroon 5 single **didn't become popular**. It was such a good song.

4 Most critics say the latest Adam Sandler movie **didn't have** "depth and soul," but I thought it was awesome.

5 Brazil was confident of winning the 2014 World Cup, but maybe this confidence **had the opposite effect**. Their team lost to Germany 7–1.

B Make it personal In pairs, share opinions on recent flops you remember. Any surprises?

A Choose two examples in A and replace the underlined words with your own opinions.
B Ask follow-up questions and continue the conversation.

books   movies   music   plays   restaurants   soccer teams   TV shows

I had high hopes for that new Turkish restaurant, but it didn't really live up to expectations. The service was great, but the food really wasn't anything special.

Common mistake

I've just streamed ~~the new John Legend's album~~. *the new John Legend album / John Legend's new album*

7 Pronunciation: Stress patterns in nouns and verbs

A 7.10 Listen to the examples from the article. Then complete with "verbs" or "nouns."

How can anyone say *no* to a **pre**sent?
Sometimes unexpected problems pre**sent** themselves.

Some words are stressed on the first syllable when they're used as ______ and on the second syllable when they're used as ______ .

B 7.11 Predict the stressed syllable in the bold words. Then listen, check, and repeat.

1 Are you in the middle of an important **project** right now?
2 Have noise, pollution, and traffic **increased** in your city recently?
3 Who's the **rebel** in your family?
4 Do you ever **record** yourself in English?
5 How much **progress** have you made with English this year?
6 When was the last time you got a **refund**?

C Make it personal In groups, ask and answer 1–6 in B. Anything in common?

It's not exactly a project, but I'm midway through my final exams. What a nightmare!

I know the feeling. How's it going?

8 Language in use

A In groups, which of the three paintings do you like most / least? Why?

I'm not sure. The da Vinci is beautiful, but there's nothing to see in the background.

I love Kahlo's hair. But the portrait itself doesn't do anything for me.

I'm not really into modern art at all. The one I like least is ...

1
Pre-impressionism

Lady with an Ermine
Leonardo da Vinci

2
Impressionism

Dancers in Blue
Edgar Degas

3
Modern

Self Portrait
Frida Kahlo

B 7.12 Listen to Rick and his friend Peter. Why is Rick worried? What does Peter suggest?

C 7.13 Read the guide and match the highlighted verbs to pictures 1–5. Listen to check. When do you do each action?

How to pretend you're ... an art expert

1 Stare thoughtfully, but don't squint as if you need glasses. Act classy.

2 Rub your chin to look intellectual, but don't scratch your head. You'll appear dumb!

3 Examine the piece closely, walk back two steps, and deliver an enigmatic "hmmm." And another one.

4 Listen carefully to the others in your group. If asked a question, frown a little, as if searching your vast mental repertoire.

5 Let the other person do most of the talking by replying with another question.

6 Learn to invent words with the prefix *meta*, meaning "of a higher order." Say, "What an interesting metaperspective!" People may look puzzled, but will probably nod in agreement.

1

2

3

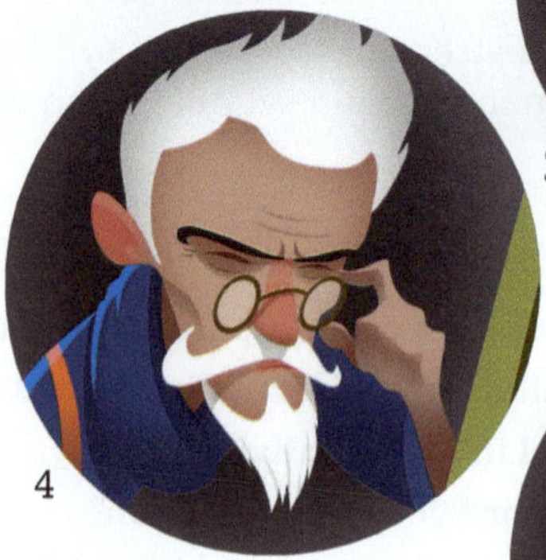
4

5

I scratch my head when it itches, or when I'm thinking.

D Make it personal In groups, answer 1–4. Anything in common?

1 What can go wrong when you try to impress people like that?
2 Would you ever date someone with completely different interests from you?
3 Do you have a favorite painting, photo, statue, or museum?
4 Have you ever pretended to be knowledgeable about something?

One day my girlfriend's dad started quizzing me on classical music. Not my specialty!

9 Grammar: Modifying nouns

A Study sentences 1–5 and check (✔) the correct rules. Find three more examples in 8C.

1 Let's look at **another** website.
2 I'd like to find **(some) other** information / opinions.
3 There must be **some other** way to do it.
4 I think **the other** advice / idea / people might be more helpful.
5 I like the first three choices, but **the others** don't appeal to me.

Modifying nouns: *Another, some other, the other,* and *the others*

What follows ...	*another?*	*some other?*	*the other?*	*the others?*
a singular noun	✔			
a plural noun				
an uncountable noun				
no noun at all				

Use ***the*** to refer back to a noun already mentioned. ***One*** is often added when the noun is singular: *Do you prefer this **photo** or **the other** (one)?*

Some in ***some other*** is not optional when nouns are ☐ singular ☐ uncountable ☐ plural.

Common mistakes

I'm sorry, I can't tonight. I have ~~another / others / the other~~ *(some) other* plans. Maybe ~~other~~ *another* time?

Grammar expansion p.150

B 7.14 Complete the extract with *another, other,* or *the others*. Listen to check. Imagine how their date ended.

SUE: This one's nice. I like it better than [1]________ .
RICK: Hmm ... Let me look at it [2]________ time. Yes, I agree. It really captures the essence of passion, conflict, and ... and some [3]________ things.
SUE: I guess.
RICK: And don't you just love his use of color? Experimental, but structured.
SUE: Err ...
RICK: [4]________ artists may try, but nobody comes close to Picasso.
SUE: But that's a Kandinsky.
RICK: Oh, yes, you're right. It's [5]________ metaperspective, isn't it?
SUE: What's that supposed to mean?

C In pairs, find another painting and adapt / role play the conversation in 9B. Role play for the class. Who sounds most like an art critic?

D Make it personal Choose the correct form. In pairs, explain each quote. Who do you agree with most?

1 "Happiness is having a large, loving, caring, close-knit family in [**another** / **other**] city." (George Burns)
2 "Each person must live life as a model for [**others people** / **others**]." (Rosa Parks)
3 "Live rich, die poor; never make the mistake of doing it [**other** / **the other**] way round." (Walter Annenberg)
4 "I believe in living on impulse as long as you never intentionally hurt [**other** / **another**] person." (Angelina Jolie)
5 "Life is what happens while you are busy making [**other** / **others**] plans." (John Lennon)

I think Annenberg is saying we worry too much about the future and don't enjoy the present.

7.5 Which musician do you listen to most?

10 Listening

A Do you recognize the musician on the right? His initials are M.D. Guess what the quote refers to, too.

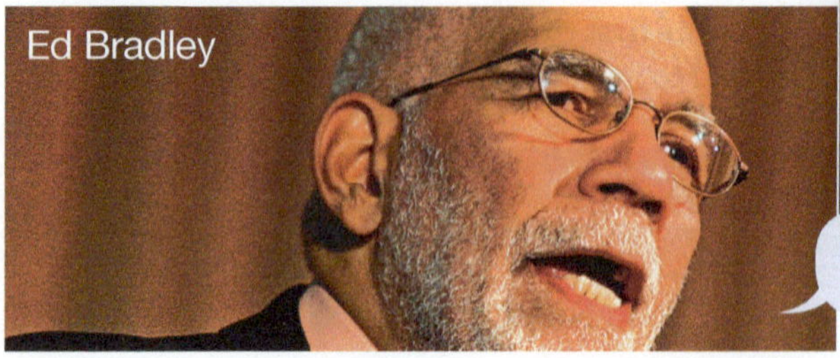

It is one of the single greatest achievements in recorded music.

B 7.15 Listen to two friends talking about *Kind of Blue*. Match the musicians to the comments (1–3). Then search *Kind of Blue* and listen to a few minutes of the album. Do you agree with these quotes?

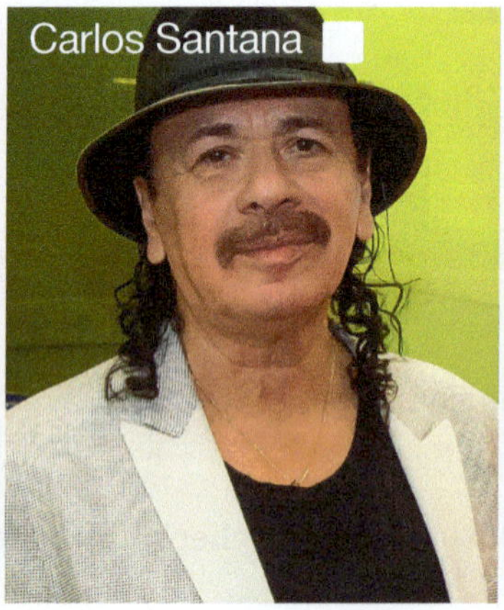

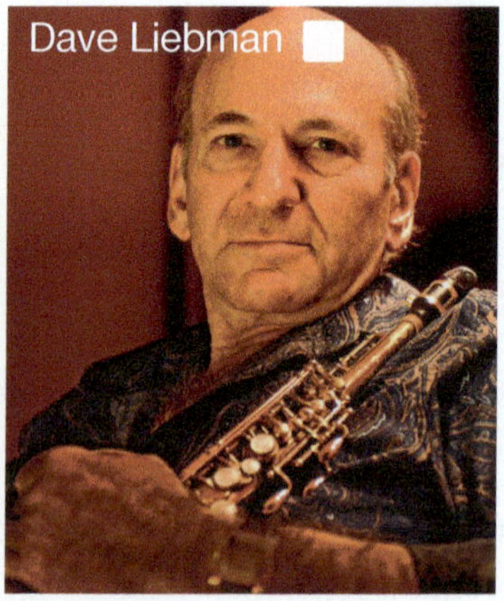

1 How do you go to the studio with minimum stuff and come out with eternity?

2 If there's one record and we've all said it, but it's true, that captures the essence of jazz for a variety of reasons, it would have to be *Kind of Blue*.

3 It's a cornerstone record, not only for jazz. It's a cornerstone record for music.

Definitely. I closed my eyes and started dreaming. Beautiful!

It's a bit slow, with no lyrics. It made me feel kind of lonely.

C 7.16 Listen to the rest of the conversation. T (True) or F (False)? Correct the false statements.

1 In the 1950s, jazz in New York City was played mainly in Harlem.
2 Jazz was so popular that players were in the media regularly.
3 Duke Ellington and Count Basie were popular before Miles Davis.
4 In the 1950s, if you liked R & B (Rhythm and Blues), you couldn't possibly like jazz.
5 Miles was the "essence of hipness" (ultra cool) because he went to Juilliard Music School.

11 Keep talking

A Choose a favorite album. Note down answers to 1–6. Search online as necessary.

1 What's the album called and who recorded it? When?
2 What type of music would you say it is?
3 What makes the music really special?
4 Which is your favorite track? Who wrote it?
5 Are there any tracks that were a letdown? Ones you usually skip?
6 Was the album commercially successful? Locally? Globally?

My all-time favorite is Ivete Sangalo's live album. It came out in 2014. Her music is so easy to dance to.

She's fun, but I'm not really into her music or the lyrics. I prefer songs with a message.

B In groups, discuss your chosen albums. Is everybody familiar with them?

12 Writing: Writing a review

A Read the review on the right and underline the answers to the questions in 11A.

B Read *Write it right!* Underline seven more examples of *-ly* adverbs in the review and mark them a–c.

Write it right!

In a review, use adverbs to make your attitude clear and your ideas more "colorful." Adverbs can modify:

a An adjective or another adverb: She has an ***amazingly*** *good* voice. *She sings* ***extremely*** *well.*

b A verb: *I* ***highly*** *recommend this album.*

c A whole idea: ***Surprisingly****, sales didn't live up to expectations.*

Common mistakes

the trumpet incredibly well.
Chris Botti plays ~~incredibly well the trumpet~~.

highly recommend his music / recommend his music highly.
I ~~recommend highly his music~~.

C Complete music review excerpts 1–8 in the most logical way. Check your spelling!

consistent	~~easy~~	unfortunate

1 This is _easily_ their best album in a decade – no doubt about it.

2 This collection is ______ awesome, from beginning to end.

3 ______ , some of the tracks leave you a bit cold.

absolute	wonderful	sad

4 I really wanted to love their live performance. ______ , I didn't.

5 I ______ adored the new CD. It exceeded all my expectations.

6 Throughout, it is fun, romantic, and has ______ written lyrics.

occasional	disappointing	consistent

7 I enjoyed this CD, but, ______ , there are only 10 tracks in the standard edition.

8 It's ______ good, from start to finish, rather than only ______ great.

She rules the world!

I've been a Beyoncé fan since 2003, when *Dangerously in Love* came out. Her last truly great album was the 2008 smash hit *I Am ... Sasha Fierce*, so I was starting to lose hope and doubt that she would ever release another masterpiece like that. Thankfully, her fifth album, *Beyoncé*, released at the end of 2013, proved me wrong.

What I love about this album is the way she cleverly experiments with different genres. There are elements of electronica, hip-hop, disco, and R&B, of course. The album starts off with *Pretty Hurts* (co-written by superstar Sia), a deeply powerful song about the pressure to look perfect. The other 14 tracks will take you on the musical journey of a lifetime, with some of the catchiest melodies you'll ever hear. My personal favorites are *Heaven* and *Rocket*, but, honestly, there's not a single letdown. And *Blue* as a finale is just a great way to end the album.

As everyone knows, *Beyoncé* was a surprise release, with zero promotion other than an Instagram® post. Incredibly, it managed to sell close to a million copies in two weeks, which I bet even *Queen Bey* herself wasn't expecting. But even more impressive is the fact that the album featured 17 music videos – something no one had ever done before.

I'm not a professional critic, but I firmly believe that *Beyoncé* is one of the best albums of the 2010s. It's mature without being boring, courageous without being forced, and entertaining without being silly. It's just the sort of album that both fans and non-fans will fall in love with.

D Your turn! Write your own review in about 200 words.

Before
Order your notes from 11A into three paragraphs, including an introduction. Then think of a conclusion.

While
Use at least four adverbs from 12C.

After
Proofread and then post your review online. Share the link with your class.

8 Has fear ever held you back?

1 Listening

A 8.1 Listen to the ad. Brainstorm other common fears and add them to the three groups in the ad.

Another real fear is that your boyfriend or girlfriend might meet someone new.

F.E.A.R. = False Evidence Appearing Real

Fear is everywhere!

- **Real fears** (losing your job, getting ill, offending people)
- **Fears we love** (scary movies, theme park rides)
- **Exaggerated or even irrational fears** (flying, public speaking, confined spaces, the dark), which can be really upsetting

Email a video to IQYP TV talking about your worst fear, and you could be invited to our groundbreaking show, *Making F.E.A.R. disappear*.

B 8.2 Listen to the beginning of three stories. What is each person afraid of? Are any of your ideas in A mentioned?

C 8.3 Listen to the full stories. Who answer(s) each question, Lucy, Rob, or Donna?

1 How long have you had this fear?
2 How did your fear begin?
3 Do you experience any physical symptoms?
4 How supportive are your family and friends?
5 What have you done to overcome your fear?

D 8.3 Listen again. In pairs, answer one question for each person.

E Make it personal Don't panic! In groups, share your fears.

1 8.4 **How to say it** Complete the sentences from the conversation. Listen to check.

Expressing fears

	What they said	What they meant
1	I'm ______ of (spiders).	I'm really afraid of ...
2	(Clowns) freak me ______ .	
3	I ______ (flying) if I can.	I'm not comfortable with ...
4	(Cockroaches) make me a bit ______ .	
5	(Dolls) don't ______ me.	I'm not afraid of ...
6	I don't ______ (bats) at all.	

2 In groups, answer a–d. Use *How to say it* expressions on p.82. Any surprises?

a What are you / others you know most afraid of?

b What have you / they tried to do about it?

c Would you ever send your own testimonial to a show like this? Why (not)?

d Do you agree with the acronym F.E.A.R.? Are most of our fears false?

2 Vocabulary: Physical symptoms of fear

A ▶8.5 Match 1–7 to pictures a–g. Listen to check. When do you feel these symptoms?

1 I get really dizzy. ☐

2 I can't breathe. ☐

3 I start to sweat. ☐

4 I burst into tears. ☐

5 I almost pass out. ☐

6 My heart starts to race. ☐

7 I get butterflies in my stomach. ☐

> My hands start to sweat on a plane when there's turbulence.

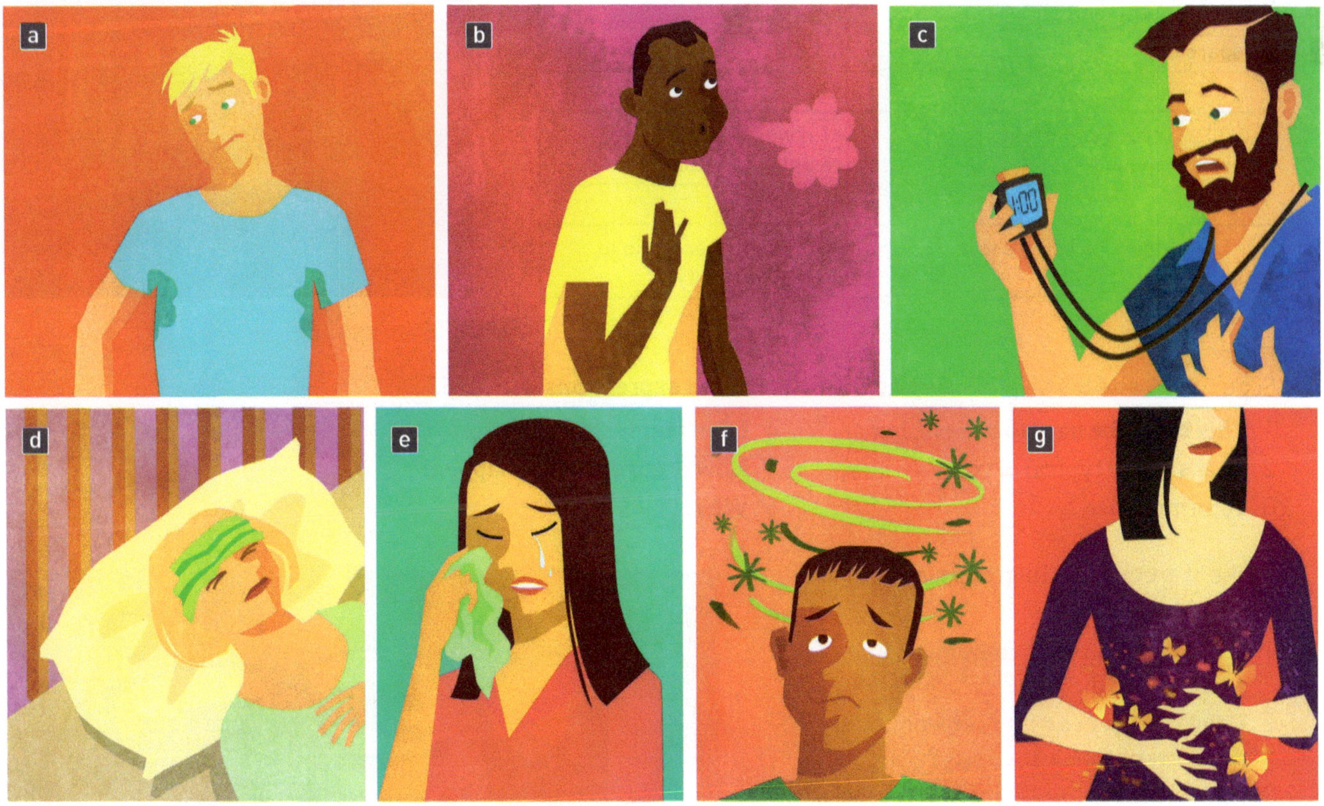

B Make it personal Share your scary experiences!

1 In pairs, share a frightening experience (true or made up!), using three expressions. Guess what is (not) true.

> I was walking home alone late one night when I heard footsteps right behind me. My heart started to race ...

2 Take turns role playing the TV show. Who's the best actor?

a Plan what to say using the questions in 1C and expressions in 1E.

b Share your fear and answer the "interviewer's" questions.

> So, welcome to *Making F.E.A.R. Disappear.* Please introduce yourself and share your fear with us.

> Hi, my name's Dan and, please don't laugh, but I'm terrified of going anywhere without my cell phone. I've felt like this for as long as I can remember, and ...

3 Language in use

A 8.6 In pairs, guess the story behind the photo. Listen to check.

I have no idea. Maybe her house was on fire.

But then she wouldn't be smiling, would she?

B 8.7 Listen to the rest of the story. Answer 1–3. Has anything like this ever happened to you?

1 Did Louise try to contact her parents?
2 Was she afraid of heights as a child?
3 Why didn't she enjoy the party?

C 8.6 and 8.7 Who said these lines, L (Louise) or D (Diego)? Order them logically as you think you heard them. Listen again to check.

[ ] [ ] I couldn't find the spare one.

[ ] [ ] So you're telling me you were able to climb the fence?

[ ] [ ] I could climb just about anything.

[L] [1] I wasn't able to get there until after 10.

[ ] [ ] I think he could see it in my eyes.

[ ] [ ] But you were able to make it to the party ...

D Scan AS 8.6 and 8.7 on p.163. Replace the underlined expressions with 1–6.

1 This might be hard to believe, but ...
2 That's really typical of you.
3 To summarize ...
4 I don't understand.
5 How often does that happen?
6 Why?

E **Make it personal** In groups, answer 1–5. Any coincidences?

1 Would you have the courage to do what Louise did?
2 Have you ever run into someone you didn't want to see at a party?
3 Name three things that are a) essential for b) can ruin a good party?
4 Are there any items you keep losing?
5 What spare items do you keep, just in case? Where do you keep them?

We keep a spare key hidden outside our apartment, in case we're locked out.

I thought of doing that, but I'm scared someone might get in.

4 Grammar: Describing past ability

A Read the grammar box and *Common mistakes*. Then check (✔) the correct answers.

Describing past ability: *could* and *was / were able to*

General	Louise **could / was able to** climb just about anything, but her friends **couldn't / weren't able to**. They weren't as athletic.
Specific occasion	She **couldn't / wasn't able to** reach her parents. Luckily, she **was able to** climb the fence and get a taxi.
Stative verbs	Her neighbors **could** see her climbing the fence. They **couldn't** understand why.

Can and *be able to* are ☐ **often** ☐ **never** interchangeable. However, to talk about ...

1 a specific past occasion in the ☐ **affirmative** ☐ **negative**, use *be able to*.

2 a past state, with verbs like *see*, *believe*, and *feel*, use ☐ **could** ☐ **was able to**.

Common mistakes

The traffic was awful. I ~~wasn't able to~~ *couldn't* believe it. But I ~~could~~ *was able to* get to work on time. Just barely!

» **Grammar expansion p.152**

B Which *be able to* sentences in 3C can be replaced by *could(n't)*?

C Correct any mistakes in the use of *could* and *be able to*.

TWO FAMOUS ESCAPES!

Before the Berlin Wall came down in 1989, people from East Germany sometimes tried to escape to the West. In 1979, for example, a man called Hans Strelczyk (1) **could** build a hot air balloon using old bed sheets, and his family (2) **was able to** drift over to the other side! Those who saw it (3) **couldn't** believe their eyes!

Alcatraz, the most legendary prison in the world, was supposedly escape-proof. However, one day, three inmates disappeared, and Alcatraz officials simply (4) **couldn't** find them. No one knows if the three men (5) **could** escape or if they jumped in the sea and drowned. My grandfather was a guard there, and he told me everything! I (6) **could** spend hours listening to his stories!

D Make it personal In pairs, answer the questionnaire, adding plenty of detail. Use expressions from 3D. Any coincidences?

R U calm and creative in a storm? | **How well do you improvise?**

Think of times when you ...

1 ran out of gas / money / clean clothes at the worst possible moment.
2 got stuck in traffic and missed something important.
3 got caught doing something you shouldn't.
4 pretended to be enjoying yourself.
5 escaped from a very difficult situation.

We both ran out of gas, and neither of us had a clue what to do.

5 Reading

A Look at the title and choose a meaning for *fear-mongering* (1–3). Read paragraph 1 of the article to check.

1 relevant safety warnings 2 scare tactics 3 strategies to deal with fear

B Guess how Lee will answer his own question at the end of paragraph 1. Then read the rest and choose his most likely answer (1–3). Underline sentences supporting your choice.

1 "No doubt it is." 2 "Not exactly." 3 "To a certain extent."

Be Afraid. Be Very Afraid:

Fear-mongering in the 21st century

By Lee Corelli

1 As part of my job as a freelance reporter, I've been practically glued to the screen lately. Here's a snapshot of my daily routine. Wake up in the morning: "New bomb scare. FBI on the alert." Go to bed: "Unemployment at an all-time high." Wake up: "Broccoli can kill you." The list is endless, and if we took all these scary stories to heart, we might never leave home again. It's no secret that in order to grab the audience's attention and boost ratings, the media rarely fails to make things look worse than they actually are. But is this kind of fear-mongering such a big deal after all?

2 ____. The fear spread by the media shapes the way we think and act, often without us being fully aware of what's really going on. The evening news reports a "worrying increase" in plane crashes, and we rethink our travel plans. It warns of a nasty new virus, and we start to wonder if leaving home without a mask on is worth the risk. We're living as if our lives were in a constant state of imminent danger. But why are we so easily influenced?

3 ____. A number of major studies have examined how our brains cope with all the negativity that surrounds us. A recent one, carried out at Ohio State University, found a significant increase in brain activity when subjects were shown negative images as opposed to positive ones. This is especially frightening in this day and age, when we're bombarded with bad news after bad news, not only on TV, but via social media, too.

4 ____. Back in the day, our grandparents only had about half a dozen TV stations to get their news from, so it was easier for them to see through cheap fear-mongering on the rare occasions they encountered it. But the media has undergone a lot of major changes in recent years, and now, with so many channels and websites, it's much harder to tell fact from fiction. In the end, we're left with a hundred different versions of the same story, wondering which ones to trust.

5 ____. The shocking images we see of war zones and natural disasters can and do inspire fear, of course, but they can also inspire action. For example, would people have mobilized so many resources to help the victims of hurricane Katrina in 2005 if the images hadn't been all over the media 24/7? Probably not. It's up to us, though, to make sure the media does not manipulate our fears in a way that's not proportional to the problem itself.

C 8.8 Match topic sentences a–d to paragraphs 2–5. Listen to check. Did the audio help you understand the text?

a The number of news channels has also greatly increased.
b All this negativity is affecting our thoughts and actions.
c But maybe there's hope, after all.
d One reason might be neurological.

D In which paragraph (1–5) does Lee make points a–f?

a ☐ There is an increase in brain activity when we see bad news.
b ☐ The media knows what kinds of stories will keep people interested.
c ☐ People don't always realize how the media influences their daily lives.
d ☐ People are more likely to help others when they can see the problem.
e ☐ Having access to many different sources of information is not always a good thing.
f ☐ TV stations were more consistent in the past.

E Make it personal In pairs, answer 1–4. Any similarities?

1 Besides fear-mongering, how else does the media boost ratings?
2 Did any recent news stories a) scare you b) shock you c) make you laugh out loud?
3 What do you trust more, TV, the radio, the Internet, or the newspapers?
4 What other institutions use scare tactics with you? Do they work?

Oh, my school, for sure. My teachers keep telling me I'll fail this year unless my grades improve.

6 Vocabulary: Common verb + noun collocations

A Read *Noticing collocations*. Then complete the mind maps with the highlighted verbs in the article.

Noticing collocations

It's easy to notice collocations when the words occur together: *We tend to* ***pay attention*** *to bad news.*
But sometimes the words appear far from each other: *This is a key* ***issue*** *that people really need to* ***address***.

1 ________ : surgery, treatment, tests, changes
2 ________ : plan, promise, task, study
3 ________ : popularity, profits, confidence, ratings
4 ________ : news, rumors, lies, fear
5 ________ : demands, stress, loss, negativity

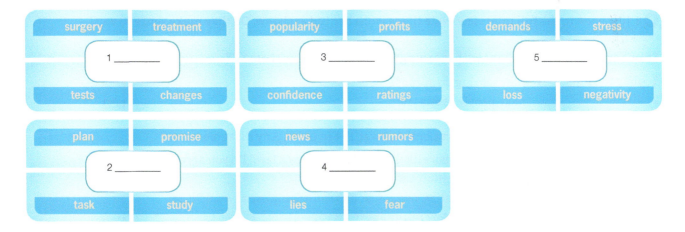

B Complete 1–5 with words from **A** in the correct form.

1 How can children ________ the ________ of a pet when it dies?
2 How different is your neighborhood from ten years ago? Has it ________ many ________ ?
3 Do you always ________ the ________ you make to friends, or do you sometimes find excuses?
4 Have you ever found out that a friend or colleague was ________ false ________ about you? What's the best way to deal with gossip?
5 What successes have you had in life? In what ways did these positive experiences ________ your ________ ?

C Make it personal Choose two questions from **B** to answer in groups. Ask for / give more details. Similar ideas?

I guess their parents should simply explain that pets die, just like people.

7 Language in use

A 8.9 Guess the missing words from an interview about the author's recent trip to Europe. Listen to check.

LAURA GÓMEZ *author of Fearless traveler*

Milan, in northern Italy, is a very happy city. So much so that you're not allowed to frown unless you're at a [1]_________ or at the hospital. Yes – smiling is required by law ... a pointless law, I know! So, if you ever visit, you'd better [2]_________ about your troubles, or else you might have to pay a fine.

In general, tourists are not supposed to eat and drink in [3]_________, but Rome has recently enforced a law banning eating and drinking at all historical sites. The fine? Up to [4]$_________! So maybe you ought to eat an extra slice of bread before leaving the hotel.

In countries like Denmark and [5]_________, driving with your headlights off is considered a violation of the law. You have to keep them on even during the day! This may sound [6]_________, I know, but you've got to obey the local laws.

B 8.10 Listen to the full interview. Note the reasons behind each law. Do they make sense to you?

C Scan **A** to find law expressions with meanings 1–4. Did you know them all?

1 obligatory
2 illegal
3 a law serving no purpose
4 make people obey a law

D **Make it personal** Crime and punishment! Answer 1–4 in pairs. Any disagreements?

1 "The heavier the punishment, the more likely we all are to obey a law." Do you agree?
2 Where you live, are some laws not enforced?
3 If you could create a new law to legalize, reward, or ban something, what would it be?
4 Search online for "stupid laws." Any funny ones?

> Here's one that says it's a violation of the law for French people to name a pig Napoleon!

8 Grammar: Expressing obligation, permission, and advice

A Match meanings 1–5 to the examples in the grammar box on p.89.

1 You (don't) have permission to do it.
2 This is(n't) an obligation. You have a / no choice.
3 My advice or suggestion: (Don't) do it.
4 My strong advice or warning: You *really* should(n't) do it, or else ...
5 People expect you (not) to do it, but it's a rule we often break.

Obligation, permission, advice: *must / have (got) to, had better, be allowed to, be supposed to,* and *should / ought to*

☐	You **must** / **have (got) to** get a visa to enter Russia.	You **don't have to** get one to go to Bermuda. Your passport will do.
☐	You**'d better** pack some warm clothes or you'll freeze!	You**'d better not** forget your coat!
☐	You**'re supposed to** keep your phone off at the theater.	You**'re not supposed to** turn it on.
☐	You **can** / **are allowed to** use computers on a plane.	You **can't** / **'re not allowed to** use them during takeoff.
☐	You **should** / **ought to** visit Times Square.	You **shouldn't** miss it.

» Grammar expansion p.152

B Circle the most logical options. Are there any laws in your country you disagree with?

1 In Saudi Arabia, you [**'re not allowed to** / **don't have to**] photograph government buildings. So you [**have to** / **'d better**] leave your camera at home – just in case you forget.

2 In France, between 8:00 a.m. and 8:00 p.m., 70% of radio music [**must** / **ought to**] be by French artists. I don't think the government [**must** / **ought to**] decide what gets played!

3 In 2013, China passed a new law saying adult children [**have to** / **are allowed to**] visit their parents. Hmm ... Maybe I [**ought to** / **must**] call my mom right now!

4 In Victoria, Australia, you [**'re not supposed to** / **'d better not**] change your own light bulbs! There's no need to be afraid, though. I doubt the police will go after you for this one.

9 Pronunciation: *have to, got to, ought to, supposed to* in informal speech

A 8.11 Listen to and repeat the examples. Notice the silent letters and schwas.

/ə/ 1 Tourists are not s~~u~~ppos~~ed~~ to eat and drink.	/f/ /ə/ 3 You ha~~ve~~ to keep headlights on.
/ə/ 2 Maybe you ou~~ght~~ to eat an extra slice of bread.	/ə/ 4 You'~~ve~~ got to obey the laws.

B 8.12 Read aloud the song lines, using informal pronunciation. Listen to check.

1 "How many times do I have to tell you, even when you're crying, you're beautiful, too." (John Legend)

2 "It's the way I'm feeling, I just can't deny, but I've got to let it go. We found love in a hopeless place." (Rihanna)

3 "Ah, but working too hard can give you a heart attack. You ought to know by now." (Billy Joel)

4 "Make me your selection, show you the way love's supposed to be." (Mario)

C Make it personal In groups, take turns personalizing 1–4. Use informal pronunciation. Who feels the guiltiest? Who has the best excuses?

Yeah, I'm guilty, I know. It's not much of an excuse, but ...

1 I know I ought to (do the laundry) more often. What's stopping me is (my dad likes doing it).

2 We have to (keep our phones off) in (class), but sometimes (I check mine quickly under my desk).

3 This week I've got to (change all my passwords). I've been putting it off for (months) because (I'm too lazy to create new ones).

4 I know I'm not supposed to (eat junk food), but I can't help it. I mean, (it tastes so good).

I know I ought to visit my grandparents more often. What's stopping me is ...

10 Listening

A 8.13 Take a test-anxiety quiz. Listen once to note down the key words from the questions. Listen again to answer each question. Then add up your score.

ANSWER ON THE FOLLOWING SCALE:

1 — 2 — 3 — 4

NOT AT ALL LIKE ME ... VERY MUCH LIKE ME

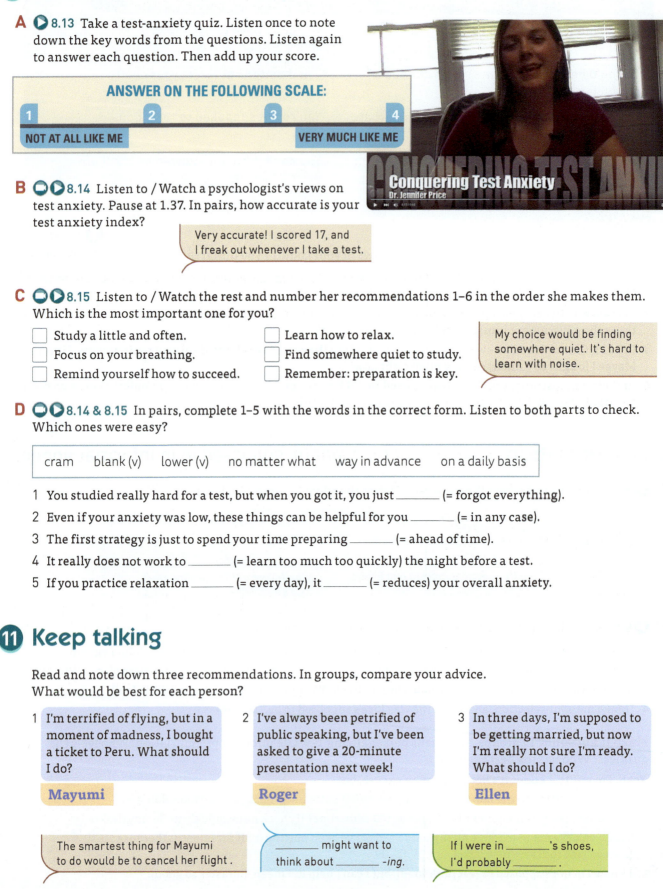

B 8.14 Listen to / Watch a psychologist's views on test anxiety. Pause at 1.37. In pairs, how accurate is your test anxiety index?

> Very accurate! I scored 17, and I freak out whenever I take a test.

C 8.15 Listen to / Watch the rest and number her recommendations 1–6 in the order she makes them. Which is the most important one for you?

- ☐ Study a little and often.
- ☐ Focus on your breathing.
- ☐ Remind yourself how to succeed.
- ☐ Learn how to relax.
- ☐ Find somewhere quiet to study.
- ☐ Remember: preparation is key.

> My choice would be finding somewhere quiet. It's hard to learn with noise.

D 8.14 & 8.15 In pairs, complete 1–5 with the words in the correct form. Listen to both parts to check. Which ones were easy?

cram	blank (v)	lower (v)	no matter what	way in advance	on a daily basis

1 You studied really hard for a test, but when you got it, you just ________ (= forgot everything).

2 Even if your anxiety was low, these things can be helpful for you ________ (= in any case).

3 The first strategy is just to spend your time preparing ________ (= ahead of time).

4 It really does not work to ________ (= learn too much too quickly) the night before a test.

5 If you practice relaxation ________ (= every day), it ________ (= reduces) your overall anxiety.

11 Keep talking

Read and note down three recommendations. In groups, compare your advice. What would be best for each person?

1 I'm terrified of flying, but in a moment of madness, I bought a ticket to Peru. What should I do?
Mayumi

2 I've always been petrified of public speaking, but I've been asked to give a 20-minute presentation next week!
Roger

3 In three days, I'm supposed to be getting married, but now I'm really not sure I'm ready. What should I do?
Ellen

> The smartest thing for Mayumi to do would be to cancel her flight.

> ________ might want to think about ________ *-ing*.

> If I were in ________'s shoes, I'd probably ________.

12 Writing: A message of advice

A Read Sonia's message to Cynthia and answer 1–3.

1 Which recommendation(s) in 10C does she mention?

2 Is there anything in Sonia's message you disagree with?

3 Which paragraph includes her most important recommendation?

B Read *Write it right!* Then match the highlighted expressions in Sonia's message to their uses 1–6.

Write it right!

When writing to someone close to you, use a variety of friendly comments to sound natural:

You shouldn't take an exam on an empty stomach. **Trust me**, it's not good for you. I did it once and almost fainted. **I mean**, I didn't literally pass out, but I came close. **Thank goodness** there was a doctor on campus.

1 Most of all, you should remember this.

2 I'm using a metaphor. Don't take my words literally.

3 Besides what I've just said ...

4 This is the first item on a list.

5 This is obvious.

6 In a way, I'm contradicting what I've just said.

Hi Cynthia,

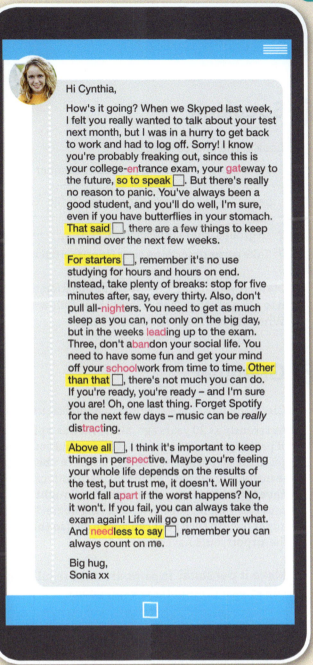

How's it going? When we Skyped last week, I felt you really wanted to talk about your test next month, but I was in a hurry to get back to work and had to log off. Sorry! I know you're probably freaking out, since this is your college-entrance exam, your gateway to the future, so to speak ☐. But there's really no reason to panic. You've always been a good student, and you'll do well, I'm sure, even if you have butterflies in your stomach. That said ☐, there are a few things to keep in mind over the next few weeks.

For starters ☐, remember it's no use studying for hours and hours on end. Instead, take plenty of breaks: stop for five minutes after, say, every thirty. Also, don't pull all-nighters. You need to get as much sleep as you can, not only on the big day, but in the weeks leading up to the exam. Three, don't abandon your social life. You need to have some fun and get your mind off your schoolwork from time to time. Other than that ☐, there's not much you can do. If you're ready, you're ready – and I'm sure you are! Oh, one last thing. Forget Spotify for the next few days – music can be *really* distracting.

Above all ☐, I think it's important to keep things in perspective. Maybe you're feeling your whole life depends on the results of the test, but trust me, it doesn't. Will your world fall apart if the worst happens? No, it won't. If you fail, you can always take the exam again! Life will go on no matter what. And needless to say ☐, remember you can always count on me.

Big hug,
Sonia xx

C Circle the correct options in Sonia's next message.

Oh, I almost forgot. On the day of the exam, here's what you should keep in mind. [1] **[For starters / Other than that]**, make sure your head is in a good place, [2] **[other than that / so to speak]**. Think positive thoughts, relax your muscles, and watch your breathing – your brain needs enough oxygen to work well. [3] **[That said / For starters]**, don't breathe too deeply or you may feel dizzy. Remember to read the instructions very carefully and [4] **[so to speak / above all]** trust your instincts – you know your stuff! Oh, and [5] **[needless to say / that said]**, keep your phone off! But I'm sure you know this. [6] **[Above all / Other than that]**, I can't think of anything else to tell you; you'll be fine!

D Your turn! Choose a person from 11. Imagine you are close friends. Write him / her a three-paragraph message in about 250 words.

Before

Rank your recommendations from most to least important.

While

Follow the model in A. In paragraph 1, introduce the problem. In paragraph 3, give your most important advice. Use at least four friendly comments.

After

Share your message with classmates. Who has the most original suggestions?

Review 4

Units 7–8

1 Speaking

A Look at the photos on p.72.

1 Note down everything you can remember about the people, using these words and expressions.

be regarded as	come out	high-profile	rise to fame	take place

2 In groups, share information. Did you remember everything?

3 Take turns describing your favorite singer and explaining why.

I used to be really hooked on ..., but now I'm into ...

B **Make it personal** Choose three question titles from Units 7 and 8 to ask a partner. Ask at least three follow-up questions for each. What did you learn about each other?

How important is music to you?

Very! I look for new songs on Spotify every day so I can keep up.

2 Grammar

A Circle the most logical words or expressions to complete the paragraph.

As recently as 20 years ago, air travel was a pleasure. But things have changed [1][**because** / **because of**] the number of passengers and increased security, and you [2][**have to** / **'re supposed to**] expect delays. Now you [3][**'d better** / **can**] get to the airport three hours in advance [4][**be supposed to** / **in order to**] catch your flight. When you go through security, you [5][**must** / **ought to**] place your carry-on liquids in a plastic bag, and in some countries, you [6][**'d better** / **have to**] take off your shoes, too. You [7][**ought to** / **'re not allowed to**] take any sharp objects on the plane, so check your carry-on luggage before leaving home. [8][**Since** / **Because of**] even a dead cell phone might be a weapon, you might have to turn your cell phone on [9][**so that** / **as**] it can be inspected. I know I [10][**'d better** / **should**] be calm at the airport, but I never am!

B **Make it personal** In pairs, are there regulations at school or at home that you disagree with? Use at least three of these expressions.

above all	for starters	needless to say	other than that	thank goodness	trust me

My roommate has too many rules. For starters, when I come in the house, I'm supposed to ...

3 Point of view

Choose a topic. Then support your opinion in 100–150 words, and record your answer. Ask a partner for feedback. How can you be more convincing?

a You think popular music used to be better: better lyrics, better melodies, better performers. OR
You think music is always changing, and today's popular music is very good.

b You think culture is important, and everyone should keep up with music, art, and literature. OR
You think people have different interests, and culture is just one of them.

c You think everyday fears can really hold people back. OR
You think everyone is afraid of something, and it's usually no big deal.

d You think the news, for the most part, is accurate and well researched. OR
You think the news is often influenced either by politics or business considerations and may not be accurate.

4 Reading

A Read the title and first sentence of the article. Choose the best answer. Then read the rest to check.

"The jazz age" probably refers to ...

1 the 1950s. 2 a time before the 1950s. 3 a time after the 1950s.

The jazz age and beyond

By the 1950s, when Miles Davis was performing in Harlem, jazz had already come into its own. The birth of jazz is generally credited to African Americans, who began migrating to the American north in the 1920s and brought their music with them to the large cities of New York and Chicago. The "roaring 20s" or "jazz age," which ended with the Great Depression, was a period characterized by rebellion. Traditions were questioned, women got the right to vote and began to work in large numbers, and a new and innovative style of dress emerged. The improvised rhythms and sounds of jazz went hand in hand with the new age.

The spread of jazz was encouraged by the introduction of large-scale radio broadcasts in 1932. From the comfort of their living rooms, Americans could now experience new and different kinds of music. Originally, there were two types of live music on the radio: concert music and big band dance music. Concert music was played by amateurs, often volunteers, whereas big band dance music was played by professionals. As commercial radio increased, big band dance music took over and was played from nightclubs, dance halls, and ballrooms. Musicologist Charles Hamm, who studied American popular music in the context of its complex racial and ethnic dynamics, described three types of jazz on the radio: black music for black audiences, black music for white audiences, and white music for white audiences. In urban areas, African American jazz was played frequently and its popularity spread.

In the early 1940s, bebop emerged, led by Charlie Parker, Dizzy Gillespie, and Thelonius Monk. This was a more serious art form that moved jazz away from popular dance music. Other types of jazz followed, including cool jazz, a melodic style that merged the traditions of African American bebop and white jazz traditions. The original cool jazz musican was Miles Davis, who released *Birth of the cool* in 1957. Jazz had reached maturity, soon to have an international following.

B In pairs, complete the word web on the kinds of jazz played on the radio.

concert music

- 1 ______ ______ **dance music**
- **nightclubs,** 2 ______ ______ **, and** 3 ______
- **black music for** 4 ______ **audiences; for** 5 ______ **audiences**
- **white music for** 6 ______ **audiences**

C Put the events in order.

- ☐ Radio helped to spread jazz in urban areas.
- ☐ Jazz gained popularity along with the innovative style of the decade.
- ☐ Miles Davis released *Birth of the cool.*
- ☐ Jazz was played down south before the migration to the north.
- ☐ Bebop, a more serious kind of jazz, developed.

5 Writing

Write a paragraph about a type of music that's important to you or a musician that you admire. Include *-ly* adverbs, such as *amazingly, surprisingly*, and *extremely*.

9 How much time do you spend on your own?

1 Listening

A 9.1 Listen to Angela and Marco. Match them to a photo 1–3. Who's more like you?

B 9.1 Match the sentence halves and write A (Angela) or M (Marco). Listen again to check. Which opinions do you agree with most?

1 People who talk the loudest ...	a ☐ happen when I think things over.
2 Group work is better than ...	b ☐ haven't been outgoing at all.
3 All my good ideas ...	c 1 always get their ideas accepted! A
4 Most great leaders ...	d ☐ love talking.
5 Introverts ...	e ☐ should be valued more.
6 The people I work best with ...	f ☐ working alone.

I definitely think it's introverts who ...

2 Vocabulary: Interacting with people

A Take the quiz. Don't check your score yet! Which situations 1–6 have you been in recently?

ARE YOU MORE OF AN INTROVERT OR AN EXTROVERT?

1 At a party, you ...
A **mingle** as much as possible.
B talk to and stick with just one person.

2 On a long plane or bus trip, you ...
A **reveal** personal information to strangers.
B stick to **small talk**.

3 When you're upset, you ...
A **open up** to a friend.
B keep things to yourself.

4 When making a hard decision, you ...
A think out loud and ask for advice.
B sit by yourself to **think** things **over**.

5 In a group meeting, you ...
A suggest lots of ideas.
B say little and **think up** ideas on your own.

6 When people discuss politics, you tend to ...
A give your opinion.
B **keep quiet**.

B 9.2 In pairs, put the highlighted words in A into three categories. Listen to check. Which are phrasal verbs?

Socializing	Sharing	Thinking

C 9.3 Read *Word order*. In pairs, decide which of 1–5 are correct. Rephrase the wrong ones. Listen to check.

1 I don't mind revealing people my phone number, but not my address.
2 I'm not really very good at thinking new ideas up. I guess I'm not very creative.
3 Whenever I have things bothering me, I always open my friends up.
4 I guess I'm more likely to keep to myself things.
5 I tend to keep quiet my opinions. I hate disagreements.

Word order

1 Some verbs only allow indirect objects with *to*: I **revealed** the answer **to him**. (Not: ~~I revealed him the answer~~.)
2 Pronouns must go between the verb and the particle in many separable phrasal verbs: I thought **it** over for a long time. (Not: ~~I thought over it~~.)
3 Objects go between the verb and the adverb: She raised **her voice** angrily. (Not: ~~She raised angrily her voice~~.)

Common mistake

on my own / by myself
I like to solve problems ~~by my own~~.

D Make it personal Find out how introverted you really are!

1 In groups, using your quiz answers, share your own preferences.

When I'm at parties, I really like to mingle. You never know who you'll meet!

2 How would you react in these situations?

a You're at a wedding where you know no one.
b A new neighbor moves next door.
c You go to a cooking class alone.
d You're sitting next to a stranger on a long bus trip.
e You go to a cafeteria for lunch, but there are no free tables.

I'd smile and speak to the first person who smiled back. But it's still hard to open up to strangers.

3 Do you agree? Who are most alike? Check your quiz score below.

QUIZ SCORE – WHAT IT MEANS

Mostly As: You're the type who has to tell people what you're thinking. You don't like spending too much time alone, either. A true extrovert.

A balance of As and Bs: You're happy being alone, but also like to socialize. You prefer to think things over before expressing your opinions. Public speaking makes you nervous, but it excites you, too.

Mostly Bs: You're a classic introvert, a "strong silent type." At social events, you look for chances to be alone. You like intimate conversations and love to read.

I'm staying in tonight
I'm staying in tonight

9.2 What behavior is rude in your culture?

3 Listening

A 9.4 What do you know about China? Look at 1–6. T (true) or F (false)? Listen to / Watch the travel advice to check.

1 You can eat before a senior person if you're told to start.
2 Don't leave a business card on the table in front of you in a meeting.
3 It's OK to hold hands, but don't kiss your wife in public.
4 China and Japan have a positive history together.
5 If you invite a translator to dinner, you don't have to pay.
6 At someone's home, your host will give you slippers that are your size.

B 9.4 Listen / Watch again. In pairs, remember the 11 behaviors to avoid. Did any surprise you?

C **Make it personal** In groups, answer 1–3. Any surprising stories?

1 How (im)polite are people from your country? What customs might be rude somewhere else?
2 When was the last time you were mistreated in a store / restaurant? What happened?
3 What is the rudest thing anyone has ever said to you? Use "bleep" for any words you don't want to repeat.

> I used to work part-time in a supermarket. And one day, a woman pointed at me and told her son, "This is why you have to stay in school!"

4 Language in use

Read the discussion forum. Underline six expressions to show annoyance or anger. Do you agree with the opinions?

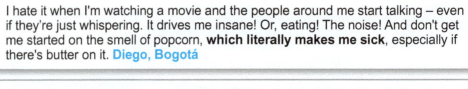

It really gets to me when I'm shopping and the employee at the checkout counter doesn't smile. I don't mean saying "thank you" or even "please," **which most of them manage to do**. I'm talking about trying to be genuinely friendly, **which is the most important thing of all**. Ji-min, Seoul

I hate it when I'm watching a movie and the people around me start talking – even if they're just whispering. It drives me insane! Or, eating! The noise! And don't get me started on the smell of popcorn, **which literally makes me sick**, especially if there's butter on it. Diego, Bogotá

It gets on my nerves when I'm riding on the bus or subway next to people whose headphones are so loud I can hear the music from several meters away. I tell you, it drives me up the wall. So I just stare at the person and start singing along, **which, strangely enough, usually does the trick**. Birgit, Munich

> Loud headphones don't bother me at all.

> Really? They drive me crazy, especially when people are singing, too. You have no idea!

5 Grammar: Uses of *which*

A Complete rules a and b with the sentence numbers (1–4). Then write a or b next to the bold examples in the discussion forum on p.96.

Uses of *which* in non-restrictive clauses

Non-restrictive clauses often reveal the speaker's opinions and feelings, as well as give information.

1 My new ringtone, **which** I love, is driving all my colleagues crazy!
2 Judy has unfriended me on Facebook®, **which** means she's probably mad at me.
3 My boss is always taking credit for people's work, **which** I think is really unfair.
4 Most of my friends like hip hop, **which** personally I can't stand.

a In sentences ______ and ______ , *which* refers to the noun before it.
b In sentences ______ and ______ , *which* refers to the whole idea before it.

Grammar expansion p.154

B 9.5 Read *Common mistakes* and correct 1–7. Listen to check. Notice the pause and the slight drop in intonation between the two clauses.

1 My car is always breaking down, this drives me up the wall.

My car is always breaking down, which drives me up the wall.

2 My WiFi signal keeps dropping every five minutes that is getting on my nerves.
3 Whenever I'm sad, my mom says "life is too short" which usually makes things worse.
4 I've been thinking of moving abroad, my friends say it's a bad idea.
5 I can't stop biting my nails what is a terrible habit, I know.
6 Yesterday, my supervisor told me to shut up that was very rude of her.
7 Today is Thursday what means I have to help with the housework.

Common mistakes

My boss is always whistling ~~what / that~~ *, which* really ~~get~~ *gets* on my nerves.

I hear message tones constantly, ~~it~~ *, which* really gets to me.

Use a comma before *which* in non-restrictive clauses, but not to separate sentences.

C In pairs, change the underlined words in **B** to make 1–7 true for you. Any unusual stories?

My cell-phone case is always coming off, which drives me up the wall.

Maybe it's time to buy a new one. Mine never comes off.

D **Make it personal** Complete the "Makes me mad!" chart. In pairs, compare ideas using *which*. Do you get annoyed by the same things?

Place / situation	Annoying habit	Your reaction
eating out	*People speak too loud.*	*It drives me insane.*
shopping		
school / work		
public transportation / driving		
home with my family		
telemarketers and call centers		

Whenever I'm eating out, people always speak too loud, which drives me insane.

Yeah, I hate that, too.

6 Reading

A Read the introduction and paragraph 1 in 6B. Then complete the dates for Generation Z. Search online to complete the chart. Which generations are the members of your immediate family from?

Generation Z: ________ to present
Millenials (Generation Y): ________ to ________
Generation X: ________ to ________
Baby boomers: 1946 to ________

> My parents were born in ... , so they must be Generation ...!

B Read the article. Complete the introduction with *better* or *worse*. Did you enjoy the interview?

THE Z FACTOR by Gloria Blanco

Already the largest generational group in the U.S., Generation Z-ers are forming a demographic tsunami that will change the country forever – and probably for the ____. Adam Smith, author of *Generating generations*, tells us why.

1 **Q:** *Why Z? I don't remember hearing that term before.*

A: It's just an arbitrary label to describe children who were born after 1997. I know that these terms don't always mean much – especially outside the U.S. – so let's call them *Screenagers*, a word coined by writer Douglas Rushkoff, which I myself [**also like better / tend to avoid**].

2 **Q:** *Interesting term.*

A: It makes perfect sense, since Generation Z kids spend over 40% of their time staring at different screens. But unlike us, *screenagers* have been using computers, tablets, and phones practically since they were born, which means that, to them, multitasking across devices [**is as natural as breathing / takes a lot of effort**]. These kids have a totally different outlook on technology than you and I do.

3 **Q:** *What else makes them unique?*

A: *Screenagers* are growing up in an unpredictable world filled with danger: extreme weather, massive poverty, endless wars and financial crises. Because of all these threats, they've developed a different attitude to risk-taking, which means they will probably seek [**more / less**] stability as adults. Also, they're fully aware of how interconnected the world is, take an interest in all kinds of social issues and are far more tolerant of diversity than I ever was. These are all very encouraging signs.

4 **Q:** *It seems they have very different priorities.*

A: Yes. In a recent study, thousands of kids were asked whether they'd rather be smarter or better looking. Nearly 70% chose "smarter," which means they seem to value [**intelligence over beauty / beauty over intelligence**] – a very welcome change, in my opinion. Just ask my thirteen-year-old! She couldn't care less about fashion, brands and accessories – unlike her older brother, who spends the whole day at the mall. No wonder they don't see eye to eye on anything!

5 **Q:** *One last question, what kind of employees will they be?*

A: Resourceful and creative, I'm sure, but with alarmingly short attention spans because of the number of distractions from their many devices, which means they'll find it [**easy / hard**] to keep focused. I'm under the impression they'll prioritize self-fulfillment over financial gains and will have a strong preference for green, socially responsible companies. Whether they'll find it easy to deal with hierarchy is hard to tell, but my philosophy has always been "rebelliousness is better than blind adherence to authority."

C Re-read. T (true), F (false) or NS (not sure)? Underline the evidence in the interview.

1 "Generation Z" is a carefully chosen term.
2 *Screenagers* will only feel comfortable with people like themselves.
3 Adam's son probably likes to wear what's in fashion.
4 Adam thinks *Screenagers* will want to have meaningful jobs that make them happy.
5 *Screenagers* will have trouble dealing with people in positions of power.
6 Adam believes authority is very important.

D 9.6 Circle the most logical option in the *which* clauses in the interview. Listen to check. Notice we stress the third syllable from the end in words ending in *-gy*, *-ty*, and *-phy*.

Pronunciation of *-gy*, *-ty*, and *-phy*

Notice we stress the third syllable from the end in words ending in *-gy*, *-ty*, and *-phy*.

psychology curiosity biography

E Make it personal In groups, answer 1–5. Similar opinions?

1 How accurately does Adam describe the *screenagers* you know?
2 Are older people necessarily wiser? Why (not)?
3 Which problems from paragraph 3 do you worry about most?
4 Do you agree with Adam's philosophy in paragraph 5?
5 Will *screenagers* have an easier life than their parents? Why (not)?

Well, I think life will be more difficult. Everything is more unpredictable and ...

7 Vocabulary: Describing attitude

A 9.7 Listen to Adam and Gloria from 6B. Label the women in her family photo a–d. In Gloria's opinion, which is more important – generation or personality?

a environmentally-aware
b happiness-seeking
c conservative
d technology-minded

B 9.8 Use the correct form of the highlighted expressions in 6B to complete 1–6. Listen to check.

1 My younger sister ________ (= is not interested in) what's going on in the world.
2 Grandma ________ (= knows) all the latest technology and enjoys using it.
3 Sometimes I ________ (= believe) that I have more in common with my grandma than with my parents.
4 My parents and I don't really ________ (= agree on) lots of things. My ________ (= attitude to) life is totally different from theirs.
5 I don't ________ (= give importance to) money and status as much as my parents do.
6 I wish my mother ________ (= open to) other people's lifestyles.

C Make it personal In pairs, modify 1–6 in B to describe people you know from different generations. Many similarities?

Most of my friends couldn't care less about politics or green issues.

Unlike me! Call me a nerd, but I watch the evening news every day!

Common mistake

~~Not like~~ Unlike you, I'm really interested in politics.

8 Listening

A 9.9 Listen to the start of an interview with a police officer. Check (✔) the correct option.

The officer thinks the robbery suspect ...

- [ ] was watching TV.
- [ ] may have hurt someone.
- [ ] was at the crime scene.
- [ ] worked at a store.

b *1*

c

B 9.10 Listen to the rest. Number the actions (1–3) in the order you hear them. There are two extra pictures.

a

d

e

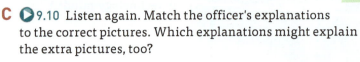

C 9.10 Listen again. Match the officer's explanations to the correct pictures. Which explanations might explain the extra pictures, too?

The suspect ...

1 [ ] wanted to run away.
2 [ ] didn't want to fall asleep.
3 [ ] was lying.
4 [ ] was making up a story.
5 [ ] was embarrassed.

D 9.11 Complete 1–6 with words from the interview, without changing the meaning. Then listen to check.

1 I questioned someone believed to have taken part in a robbery.	=	I questioned someone s*uspected of* taking part in a robbery.
2 A guy saying he was at home was the key suspect.	=	A guy c________ he was at home was the key suspect.
3 He said he wasn't involved.	=	He d________ being involved.
4 He said it was true, but it wasn't.	=	He wasn't t________ the t________ .
5 What showed the most that he was lying was ...	=	What g________ him a________ the most was ...
6 It's a story you're inventing.	=	It's a story you're m________ u____ .

E **Make it personal** Crime time! Work in pairs.

1 Use only the pictures and the words in D to remember the lies.
2 Are you good at spotting a liar? What unusual crime stories have you heard?

I once heard a story where a guy was suspected of ... He claimed ...

9 Grammar: Reduced relative clauses

A Study the sentences and complete the rules. Then find an active and a passive example of reduced relative clauses in 8D.

Reduced relative clauses: active and passive

Relative clauses can be reduced:

Active	Students	who cheat / cheating	on their final exams will not graduate.
	A passenger	(who was) riding	on the train robbed the conductor.
Passive	Anyone	(who is) caught	cheating will be suspended.
	The conductor	(who was) robbed	last night is very upset.

1 If a relative clause refers to a subject, you can delete ☐ only the pronoun ☐ the pronoun and *be*.

2 A(n) ☐ active ☐ passive verb in a reduced clause is always an *-ing* form and a(n) ☐ active ☐ passive one is always a past participle.

» Grammar expansion p.154

B Rewrite these signs with reduced relative clauses to make them more natural. Where might they appear?

1 LUGGAGE THAT'S LEFT UNATTENDED WILL BE REMOVED AND DESTROYED.

2 $20,000 REWARD FOR INFORMATION THAT LEADS TO AN ARREST.

3 ANYONE WHO IS SUSPECTED OF ENTERING WILL FACE SERIOUS CONSEQUENCES.

4 THOSE WHO ARE CAUGHT LITTERING WILL BE FINED.

5 CARS THAT ARE MOVING AT EXCESSIVE SPEEDS WILL BE IDENTIFIED BY RADAR.

6 PROTESTERS WHO ARE HOLDING UP TRAFFIC WILL BE ARRESTED.

7 ANYONE WHO SWIMS HERE WILL BE IN FOR AN UNPLEASANT SURPRISE!

1 Luggage left unattended will be removed and destroyed. You might see it in an airport or a bus station.

C Cross out all optional words in these relative clauses. If no words can be crossed out, write "none."

1 The man who was sitting next to me on the bus was very suspicious-looking.
2 People are always pushing against my seat in airplanes, which is incredibly annoying.
3 That's the place that I told you about that said "No pets or children allowed."
4 The girl who was accused of taking my notebook totally denied it.
5 I'm always stepping on gum, which drives me up the wall.

D Make it personal You're under arrest! In groups, role play a trial.

1 List five behaviors you'd like to change or ban. Use ideas from 5D on p.97 or think up others.
2 Create signs for each one. Include the penalty.
3 **A** You're a police officer. Accuse **B** of violating the law.
B Defend yourself. Explain why you did nothing wrong.
C You are the judge. Guilty or innocent? Make a fair decision.

SCHOOL
THOSE CAUGHT SPEEDING IN FRONT OF THE SCHOOL WILL DO 500 HOURS OF COMMUNITY SERVICE!

But Officer, I was only making a left turn ...

10 Listening

A 9.12 In pairs, explain the cartoon. Then listen to two students and choose the correct option.

Laura [**agrees** / **disagrees**] with Alfredo that consumerism is a serious problem.

B 9.13 Listen to and order Alfredo's ideas 1–5. Which one(s) do you agree with?

Consumerism is a problem because ...

- ☐ it has an impact on the planet's resources.
- ☐ it affects people's relationships.
- ☐ people end up overspending.
- ☐ people buy things just to feel better.
- ☐ buying things doesn't bring long-term happiness.

I definitely agree that ...

C 9.14 Listen and note down two solutions to B. Any other possible ones?

D 9.15 Listen again to excerpts from the conversation. Number them 1–4.

Alfredo's purpose is to ...

- ☐ begin to build an argument.
- ☐ explain an idea in a different way.
- ☐ try again to persuade Laura to accept his point of view.
- ☐ tell Laura she doesn't understand his argument.

11 Keep talking

A 9.16 **How to say it** Complete the chart. Then listen, check, and repeat, copying the intonation.

Developing an argument (3)

	What they said	What they meant
1	That's a ____ question.	It's hard to answer that question.
2	Why (people think it's a problem) is ____ me.	I don't understand why ...
3	There's ____ to it than that.	It's not so simple.
4	Wouldn't you ____ that (it's just a quick fix)?	Don't you think that ...
5	I know what you're ____ at.	I know what you're trying to say.

B **Make it personal** Choose a problem from the survey. Note down (a) why it's serious and (b) what could be done to solve it.

What's the biggest problem facing society today?

Our readers' top picks:
1 social injustice
2 selfishness
3 overpopulation
4 lack of respect for nature
5 corruption
6 urban violence
7 prejudice
8 unemployment
9 hyperconnectedness

C In groups, compare ideas. Use *How to say it* expressions. Where do you (dis)agree?

Hmm ... that's a tough question, but to me, the biggest problem we face today is corruption.

What makes you say that?

Well, for one thing ...

12 Writing: A problem-solution essay

A Read Alfredo's essay. Which ideas in 10B and C are mentioned?

B Read *Write it right!* Then put a–h back into the essay. There are two extra words or phrases.

Write it right!

In essays, use a variety of conjunctions to connect your ideas well. Refer back to lessons 4.2 and 7.2, too.

Purpose: (a) *in order to*, (b) *so that*

Comparing: (c) *while*, (d) *unlike*

Conceding (*but* ...): (e) *although*, (f) *despite*

Reason: (g) *as*, (h) *due to*

C Which conjunctions (a–h) could be replaced by these?

1 as opposed to *unlike*
2 since ________
3 because of ________
4 so ________
5 even though ________
6 to ________
7 in spite of ________
8 whereas ________

D In which paragraph (1–5) does Alfredo ...

- [ ] define the problem?
- [ ] offer more supporting arguments?
- [ ] conclude his argument?
- [ ] put the problem in a historical perspective?
- [ ] propose possible solutions?

E **Your turn!** Choose a problem from the survey in 11B and write a five-paragraph essay in about 280 words.

Before

Note down problems and solutions. Follow the structure in D to order them logically.

While

Write five paragraphs following the model in A. Search online for facts, as necessary. Use at least four conjunctions from B and C.

After

Post your essay online and read your classmates' work. What was the most popular problem? Similar solutions?

1 Think about the last time you wanted something *badly* – say, new designer sunglasses. When you got them, you felt great. As time went on, the sunglasses probably lost most of their initial appeal. And then you lost them and regretted spending so much in the first place! Sound familiar? Blame it on consumerism, a cultural phenomenon that encourages us to find happiness by buying what we don't need. In other words: "Buy, use, discard, buy more."

2 Consumerism is not a new phenomenon. It had its origins in the Industrial Revolution. What's new is that in today's world, partly ________ globalization, whole societies are organized around the need to consume. Some studies, for example, have found that, ________ the recent bad economy, people in the U.S. spend 100 billion dollars every year on shoes, jewelry, and watches – more than what they invest in higher education.

3 It's a mistake to believe that material possessions can make us feel better. Many studies show that focusing on owning things can lead to anxiety and even depression. Also, consumerism can affect our self-esteem, ________ it encourages us to compare ourselves with others. Finally, the worst environmental problems we face have been caused by consumerism. ________ solve them, we must confront consumerism whenever we can.

4 It's hard to escape materialism, but it's not impossible. Here's a small first step: The next time you buy something, ask yourself "Do I need it?" rather than "Do I want it?" Also, be clear about what *really* matters to you. In other words, concentrate on the things that, ________ shopping, can bring long-term happiness – your family? your career? an important cause? a new challenge? Then, instead of going to the mall, focus your energy on those things.

5 Having a less materialistic lifestyle – and ultimately saving the planet – doesn't mean giving up on life's pleasures. It simply means giving less importance to material possessions ________, over time, they become less and less important to you.

10 How do you like to get around town?

1 Listening

A In pairs, read the ad and take turns guessing the problems. Then add four more.

A Mime a problem.

B Guess what it is.

> From your expression and gestures, that must be annoying kids!

B 10.1 Listen to three friends, Joel, Ana, and Ian. Which travel nightmare in **A** is each talking about?

C 10.2 Guess how each story ends, picture A or B. Listen to check. Did you get them all right?

the Travel blog

THIS WEEK: TRAVEL NIGHTMARES

We've all been there: road rage, flat tires, running out of gas, (near) crashes, reservation problems, cancelations, missed connections, annoying kids, unpleasant fellow travelers ...

The list goes on and on. Do you have a tale to tell? Click here to tell us about your worst travel experience ever!

Story 1 Story 2 Story 3

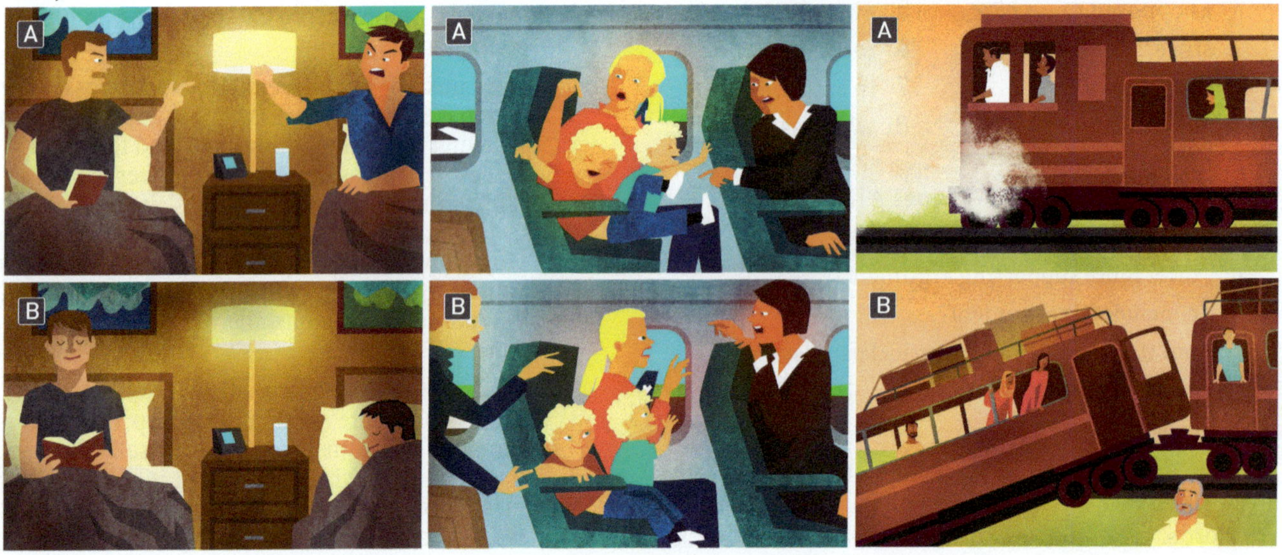

D 10.2 Listen again. T (true), F (false) or NI (no information)? Whose story was the most surprising?

1 John was afraid at first that Barry couldn't be trusted.
2 John and Barry didn't talk about work.
3 When Ana saw the twins on the plane, she was sure they'd misbehave.
4 She asked them not to kick her seat, several times.
5 The conductor left the train to get something to eat.
6 Ian says he was never in real danger.

E Make it personal Which quotes 1–5 are good advice for Joel, Ana, or Ian? Which ones do you like best?

1 "Once a year, go someplace you've never been before." (Dalai Lama)
2 "Everything is funny as long as it's happening to someone else." (Will Rogers)
3 "You get educated by traveling." (Solange Knowles)
4 "When traveling with someone, take large doses of patience and tolerance with your morning coffee." (Helen Hayes)
5 "Wherever you go becomes a part of you somehow." (Anita Desai)

> Ana seems to work hard. Maybe the first one is good for her.

> And me! I wish I had the money to travel, though!

2 Vocabulary: Phrasal verbs

A 10.3 Read the definitions and complete 1–6 with the correct phrasal verb. Listen to check. Then, in pairs, use only the pictures in 1C to remember each story.

dawn on: To begin to be perceived or understood. *It only dawned on me that I could actually speak English when I finally went abroad.*

end up: Eventually arrive at a place or situation. *When shopping, I always end up spending more than I ought to. My parents say I'll end up with a huge credit card debt.*

get away: To escape. *College is driving me crazy. I wish I could get away for a week or so.*

get through: To manage to deal with or survive a difficult experience. *If I lived in Canada, I'd find it very difficult to get through winter there. I hate the cold!*

look forward to: To await eagerly or anticipate with pleasure. *I'm really looking forward to (watching) this year's Super Bowl.*

mix up: To confuse two people or things, or spoil the arrangement of something. *My closet is a mess! My winter clothes are all mixed up with my summer clothes.*

1 I was really ________ relaxing after a long flight.
2 How did you manage to ________ a whole week with that guy?
3 The poor man probably got ________ and pulled the wrong switch.
4 When it finally ________ the passengers that they were in trouble, everyone started screaming.
5 It'd been a rough year and all I wanted was to ________ from it all for a few days.
6 The woman got really mad, and we ________ arguing.

Joel had just flown from Washington to London, and he was really looking forward to relaxing after a long flight ...

B In pairs, modify the examples in A so they are true for you. Anything in common?

It only dawned on me how hungry I was when I ...

Common mistakes

I'm not really looking forward to ~~meet~~ *meeting* my in-laws. What if they end up ~~dislike~~ *disliking* me?

C Make it personal Describe your worst travel nightmare ever.

1 10.4 **How to say it** Complete the sentences from 1B and C. Then listen to check.

Talking about unexpected events

	What they said	What they meant
1	It ________ out (the hotel had made a mistake).	In the end, it proved to be true that ...
2	I ________ to (know who the man was).	By chance, I ...
3	For whatever ________, (the conductor stepped off the train).	No one knows why ...
4	As ________ would have it, (they were able to stop the train).	Luckily, ...
5	In the end, strangely ________, (it wasn't nearly as bad as I thought).	It may seem strange, but ...

2 Plan or make up your story. Use the travel nightmares in 1A to help you.

a Note down the main events. Ask yourself *what, when, where, why,* and *how?*
b Include three or more a) phrasal verbs and b) *How to say it* expressions.
c In groups, tell your stories. Whose experience was the most unpleasant?

I've got to tell you what happened on my vacation last year ...

3 Listening

A 10.5 Marty Falcon is on vacation. Listen and match the start of three conversations to three of the pictures (a–d). How does his tone suggest he is feeling?

To me, it sounds like he wants to go home!

a

b

c

d

B 10.6 Listen to the full conversations. Check (✔) all the statements that can be inferred. Have you ever had / heard of a tourist experience like this?

1 Marty ...
- ☐ wants to leave the hotel and go straight to the airport.
- ☐ won't take no for an answer.

2 The salesperson ...
- ☐ has no idea if the pants will shrink.
- ☐ agrees they're expensive.

3 Marty ...
- ☐ hasn't used the app before.
- ☐ stopped the car as soon as he noticed the light.

Well, it didn't happen to me personally, but a friend of mine went to ... and ...

Common mistake

a friend of ~~me / him / her~~ *mine / his / hers*

4 Pronunciation: Word stress in nouns and phrasal verbs

A 10.7 Read *Nouns from phrasal verbs* and listen to the examples. Check (✔) the correct rule.

Nouns from phrasal verbs

Some nouns formed from phrasal verbs are hyphenated; others are written as one word.

- I was wondering if I could get a late **checkout** (n) tomorrow. I need a **wake-up call**, too.
- Sorry, you need to **check out** (v) by noon. Just dial 00. The system will **wake** you **up**.

The stress in most phrasal verbs is on the ☐ **verb** ☐ **particle**.
The equivalent nouns are usually stressed on the ☐ **first** ☐ **second** part of the word.

B 10.8 Underline the stressed syllables in the bold words. Listen to check. Then find three comments in AS 10.6 on p.163 that show Marty is an inexperienced traveler.

1 Almost 100 dollars? That's a **rip-off**! Aren't these things supposed to cost about 20 bucks?
2 My car **broke down** and I don't know what to do! I'm lost in the middle of nowhere.
3 The fastest way to report a car **breakdown** is via our app. Do you know whether you have it installed on your phone?
4 Yeah, but I don't have a **login** or a password. Can't you help me over the phone?
5 It seems there's been a **mix-up**. Let me see if I can correct it and **fix** things **up**.

C **Make it personal** Complete 1–3 with words from **B**. Then ask and answer in pairs. Any good stories?

1 When was the last time you said, "I got confused. Sorry for the ________"? What happened?
2 Is 500 dollars for a watch a fair price or a ________ ? How much would you be willing to pay? Do you ever feel you're being overcharged when you shop?
3 What would you do if your car ________ late at night and your phone was dead?

I'd be terrified if there was no one around! I guess I'd lock the doors and wait until it got light.

5 Grammar: Negative and indirect questions

A Read the grammar box and check (✔) the correct rules 1–3. Then in 4A and B, underline two indirect questions and circle two negative questions.

Negative questions; indirect questions: *Wh-* and *yes-no*

Use negative questions when you expect a positive answer:
Isn't there free WiFi? Yes, the network name is "guest123."
Don't I have until noon to check out? Well, no, actually, checkout is at 11:00.

Use indirect questions to soften the tone of your questions or requests:
Where**'s** the nearest ATM? → **Do you (happen to) know** where the nearest ATM **is**?
What time **does** the gym **close**? → **Could you tell me** what time the gym **closes**?
Did anyone **leave** me a message? → **I'd like to know if / whether** anyone **left** me a message.

1 Use ☐ **full** ☐ **contracted** forms to start negative questions. Answer yes to confirm them.
2 Indirect questions ☐ **have** ☐ **don't have** the same word order as statements.
3 The word *If* ☐ **can** ☐ **can't** be replaced by *whether.*

» Grammar expansion p.156

Common mistakes

Do you know how long ~~does it take~~ *it takes* to get there?
Could you tell me where ~~are the restrooms~~ *the restrooms are*?

B ▶ 10.9 Correct the mistakes in 1–5. Listen to check. Then, in pairs, use only the pictures in 3A and questions to role play each dialogue in 3B.

1 Can you tell me what time will she be back?
2 Would you happen to know are these machine-washable?
3 Cannot you help me over the phone?
4 Do you remember did any warning lights come on?
5 Do you know what is your exact location?

C Annoying questions! Turn 1–5 into indirect questions. Then complete the follow-up negative questions.

	Annoying question	Annoying follow-up question
At a hotel	1 Did anyone ever die in this room? (Do you happen to know ...?)	No idea? _____ you check with your manager? Please?
On a flight	2 Is this gluten-free? (Can you check ...?)	Really? _____ there a gluten-free option?
At home	3 How much have you spent on shoes this year? (Do you have any idea ...?)	Wow! _____ you have enough shoes already?
At a language school	4 How long will it take me to speak fluent Chinese? (I'd like to know ...)	That long? _____ there a miracle method or something?
At a store	5 Could you help me, please? (I wonder ...)	_____ the other customer wait?

D Make it personal Be annoying! In pairs, role play and expand two situations in C. Include indirect and negative questions. Then present one to the class and vote on the funniest.

Can't the customer wait? I'm important, too!

Please be patient, sir ... what can I do for you?

This phone is driving me nuts. Could you tell me how I turn it on?

10.3 Which foreign country would you most like to live in?

6 Reading

A Read paragraph 1 of Arturo's blog. Use the photo to guess his nationality and answer 1 and 2.

1 Was the party in the U.S. or his country of birth?

2 Which five habits did he change when he went abroad?

B Read paragraph 2. Check (✔) the true statement(s). Is the story interesting so far?

Arturo ...

☐ got a degree abroad.
☐ was starting to lose touch with friends.
☐ found it easy to adjust when he returned home.
☐ sometimes questions his decision to live abroad.

C Read the rest. How would he answer the last question in paragraph 2?

☐ absolutely ☐ not really ☐ not at all

WINDS OF CHANGE

HOME | ABOUT | ARTICLES | CONTACT

1 Two years ago I was at a birthday party when an old friend called my name. It went in one ear and out the other. "Arturo? Are you deaf?" he repeated. For a split second, I didn't recognize Arturo as my name! I'd grown so used to being called Art by my American friends that now, back home, my birth name sounded as if it belonged to somebody else. That was the first time I'd experienced reverse culture shock; that is, culture shock not from going abroad, but from coming back. Other symptoms followed, of course: being more punctual than anyone else, driving more slowly, eating earlier, giving better tips, telling fewer jokes – you name it. What was going on with me?

2 I'd just returned from doing an MA in San José, CA, in information technology. I was thrilled to see my family and reconnect with all the friends I'd left behind and was beginning to drift apart from. I was also looking forward to going back to work so I could put all the theory I'd learned into practice. I wanted to get on with my old life in Madrid, but something was missing and I couldn't put my finger on what. Strangely enough, after all this time, I still can't. My time in the U.S. is still a powerful magnet that constantly pulls me back to all the sights, the smells, and the little joys and annoyances of the life I left behind. I think I'm finally coming to terms with the fact maybe I'll never have a clear sense of home again, which sometimes makes me wonder: was my time abroad worth it?

3 Studying or working abroad, trying to express your personality in another language, and fitting into a different culture can be frustrating, especially at first. You have to get used to both being and sounding foreign, and you have to grow to like your new self – your new identity. But here's the good news: Your self-awareness develops, and your outlook on life changes. Many of your old pre-conceived ideas crumble like buildings in an earthquake. You learn that "normal" means socially acceptable in different cultures – nothing more than that. And, most of all, you finally begin to remove all the labels that had come to define you. At home, people always thought of me as the family genius, but back in California I was just "the nice guy from Madrid," which means I can be whoever I choose to be.

4 When you move abroad, you're forced to abandon your roots and take a leap into the unknown. Things can and do go wrong, but you learn that you can get through the rough times without your family. You also realize that the ugly haircut or the wrong meal you got because of your limited vocabulary, at the end of the day, mean absolutely nothing. And, most of all, you realize that – pardon the cliché – you become a better person. Not better than those around you, but definitely better than your former self, no matter where you are – "home" or otherwise.

D Does Arturo make these points in paragraph 3 or 4?

When you live abroad, you ...

☐ become more accepting of diversity.
☐ learn to rely more on yourself.
☐ can reinvent yourself.
☐ don't get bothered by small problems.

E ▶10.10 Try to pronounce the pink-stressed words. Listen to check. Did you get all the vowels right?

F **Make it personal** In groups, answer 1–5. Any surprises?

1 Which benefit(s) of living abroad in 6D would be most important to you? Can you think of any others?
2 If you could spend a year abroad, where exactly would you go and why?
3 Would you prefer to move abroad or to another place in your own country? Why?
4 If you moved abroad, would it bother you having a foreign accent?
5 Which aspects of your identity might be hardest to abandon?

> I think I'd miss my hometown most of all. After all, I've lived here since I was born. It's part of my identity.

7 Vocabulary: Words with literal and figurative meanings

A Match the words to the pictures 1–6.

crumble	fit	label	leap	magnet	root

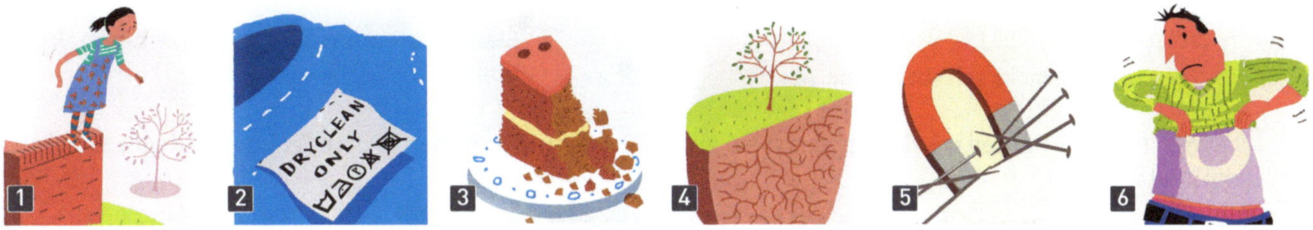

B Read *Literal or figurative?* Then match the highlighted words in Arturo's blog to the definitions 1–6. Do you know any other words with figurative meanings?

> **Literal or figurative?**
>
> Words can have literal (concrete) or figurative (abstract) meanings. Knowing a word's literal meaning can help you guess what it means when it's used figuratively:
> My older sister was scared to **dive** into the pool (literal) / into a new relationship (figurative).

1 *fitting* : being in harmony with or belonging to
2 ______ : origins or source
3 ______ : arbitrary description or identifying words
4 ______ : make a sudden change or transition
5 ______ : fall apart or break down completely
6 ______ : a force that attracts

C Complete 1–6 with the correct form of the words in A.

1 Think of a ______ often attached to your country or city. Do you think it's a fair description?
2 How's the economy doing in your country? Is it in good shape, so-so, or ______ ?
3 "Money is the ______ of all evil." Do you agree?
4 Some people seem to be a ______ for bad luck or trouble. Do you know anyone like that?
5 Can you think of an artist that successfully made the ______ from music to movies?
6 At school, how hard do / did you try to ______ in with the "cool kids" in your class?

D **Make it personal** In pairs, choose three questions in C to answer. Any surprises?

> Well, Montevideo is known as "a culinary paradise" because our meat and fish are so good. Of course!

8 Language in use

A 10.11 Listen to the start of a podcast. Who is being interviewed and why?

B 10.12 Listen and order the photos 1–5. Who do you think is having the hardest time?

C 10.12 Listen again. T (true) or F (false)?

1 Mariana had a sedentary lifestyle in Venezuela.
2 Ignacio mostly blames his roommate for their cold relationship.
3 Ines says she lacks self-discipline.
4 Diego found it hard to adapt to life in the U.S.
5 Elena's parents are going to take her back home.

D Match the highlighted words in podcast excerpts 1–5 to definitions a–f. Which feelings and opinions can you relate to?

1 I was born and raised in Caracas, so I kind of miss the **hustle and bustle** of life there. ... I'm sure I'll get used to the peace and quiet eventually.
2 I'm not used to sharing a room with anyone – **let alone** someone I **barely** know.
3 Here we have regular assignments, quizzes, projects, and exams, which can be a little **overwhelming**. I wonder if I'll ever get used to working this hard.
4 When I came here, I was used to life in the States. I mean, there was less of a culture **clash** than I'd anticipated.
5 I started to feel terribly **homesick**. I wasn't used to being away from my parents for more than a couple of days.

a a conflict ____________
b much less, not to mention ____________
c noisy, energetic activity *hustle and bustle*
d scarcely, hardly ____________
e sad because you're away from home and family ____________
f so confusing and difficult, it's hard to deal with ____________

> I can definitely relate to the last one. I felt so homesick when I ...

E **Make it personal** How would you feel about leaving home to study or work?

1 Do you make new friends easily?
2 Are you a good roommate? How many people have you shared an apartment or dorm with? Have you had good experiences?
3 Would you mind sharing a kitchen and a bathroom? Is there anything you couldn't share?
4 How badly would you miss your family? How often would you contact them?
5 How often do you need peace and quiet? What do you do to find it?

> Well, I actually went away to school. The first year was a nightmare because ...

9 **Grammar:** Talking about acquired habits

A Read the grammar box. Check (✔) T (true) or F (false) in rules 1 and 2.

Talking about acquired habits: *be* and *get used to*

be used to **(the state)**	***get used to*** **(the process)**
Ignacio **isn't used** to sharing his room.	He'll have **to get used to** it.
Diego **was** already **used to** living abroad.	He still **hasn't gotten used to** the weather.
Ines **is** still **not used to** college life.	She'**s** slowly **getting used to** doing more homework.

1 ***Be used to*** means *be accustomed to* and ***get used to*** means *become accustomed to.* ☐ T ☐ F
2 After ***be / get used to***, you can use a verb in the *-ing* form or a noun. ☐ T ☐ F

Grammar expansion p.156

Common mistakes

I ~~use to wake~~ *'m used to waking* up early. But I'll never ~~used to go~~ *get used to going* to bed late.
How often did you ~~used~~ *use* to go skiing when you lived in Argentina?

B 10.13 Correct the mistakes in 1–3. Listen to check. Notice the /s/ sound in *used*.

1 Mom says we'll get used to live together.
2 I'm not used to been treated as an adult.
3 It took me a while to used to the weather.

C In pairs, use only the photos in **8B** to remember all you can about each person. Check in **AS** 10.12 on p.163. Anything you missed?

D Complete 1–4 with *be* or *get* in the correct tense. Then complete 5–7 with a form of the verbs in parentheses.

TOUGH CHANGES!

	Marco, from Colombia: moving out of your parents' house	Kathleen, from Denver: selling your car and buying a bicycle
a Was it tough at first?	I come from a large family, so at first I (1) _____ used to the silence. I found it really weird.	Not as hard as I thought. I used to (5) _____ (ride) my bike everywhere when I lived in Amsterdam, which certainly helped.
b Any other problems?	It took me a long time (2) _____ used to doing all the housework by myself because I (3) _____ used to having a housekeeper.	Not really. I don't mind the effort. I go to the gym every day, so I'm used to (6) _____ (work) out.
c How are things now?	I guess I'm slowly (4) _____ used to being on my own, and I kind of like it.	I've gotten so used to (7) _____ (go) to work by bike, I don't think I'll ever need a car again.

SEARCH OUR ARCHIVE:
changing schools / getting into college / getting married / moving to a new city / becoming a vegetarian / starting an exercise program / switching from iOS to Android (or vice versa!)

E **Make it personal** Choose a topic from the website in **D**, answer questions a–c mentally, and make notes. Then, in pairs, interview each other. Who had the hardest time adapting?

I started college last year, and it was a bit of a shock at first.

What was hard about it?

Well, I was used to smaller classes and ...

10 Listening

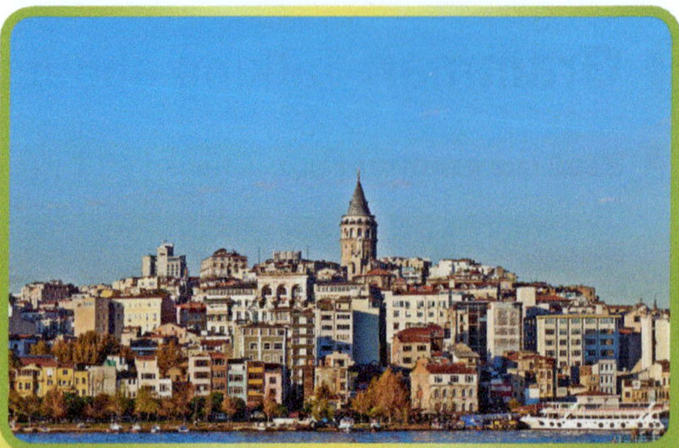

A 10.14 Take the quiz. T (true) or F (false)? Listen to check. How many correct guesses?

How much do you know about Istanbul?

1. Istanbul is one of the five largest cities in the world.
2. Two-thirds of the city is located in Europe and one-third in Asia.
3. Istanbul's subway is the oldest in the world.
4. As the city is surrounded by water, it doesn't snow there.
5. Over time, it has been the capital of three different empires.
6. The Grand Bazaar is the world's most visited tourist attraction.

B 10.15 Listen to Bill and Gail's first impressions of Istanbul and answer 1 and 2.

1. List three reasons why Bill loves Istanbul.
2. List three things you can do there. Would you like to visit the city?

C 10.16 Listen to the second part. T (true), F (false), or NI (no information)? Have you been anywhere at all like this?

1. The Grand Bazaar is smaller than a city block.
2. Bill thinks The Grand Bazaar is still getting bigger.
3. You can buy rugs, slippers, and jewelry.
4. According to the conversation, you can also buy live animals.
5. It's less crowded early in the morning.

D 10.17 Complete 1–5 with the correct prepositions. Use your intuition! Listen to check. Any surprises?

1. I can't wait to explore the city ___ the next few days.
2. We should definitely stock up ___ these for an afternoon snack or two.
3. And then we can go ___ some Turkish ice cream.
4. Istanbul is love ___ first sight, isn't it?
5. It [the Grand Bazaar] is one of the largest markets ___ the entire world.

11 Keep talking

A What's the most amazing place you've ever been / imagined going to? Think through 1–7. Search online, if necessary.

1. What's it called and what country is it in?
2. Is it historically significant in any way?
3. When did you first go (first imagine going) there?
4. What was your first reaction to the place?
5. What are the highlights? What else is there to do?
6. Did you need to take any precautions?
7. Have you been back there since (or in your dreams)? How many times?

B In groups, describe the places. Be sure to answer 1–7. Which sounds the most irresistible?

I think Rio is the most unbelievable place I've ever been.

Oh, I'd love to go. What's so special about it?

Well, as you know, it's famous for Sugarloaf Mountain ...

12 Writing: A travel report

A Read Lucy's travel report. Does it make you want to visit both places? How many times has she been there?

B Write the question numbers 1–7 in 11A next to each paragraph A–E.

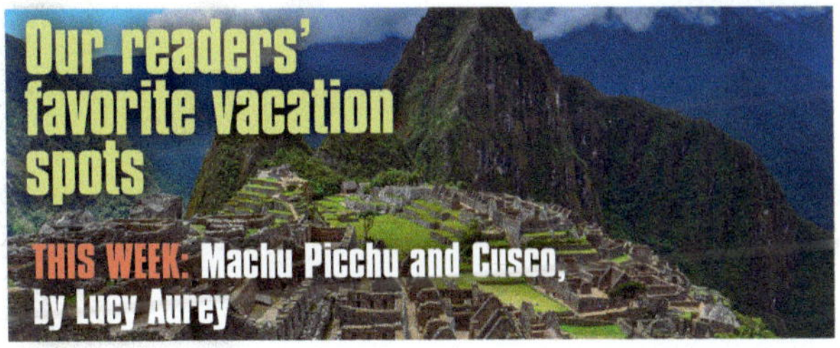
Our readers' favorite vacation spots
THIS WEEK: Machu Picchu and Cusco, by Lucy Aurey

A I was twelve when I first learned that Machu Picchu, which means "old mountain," is Peru's most popular tourist attraction and one of the world's most famous archeological sites. The textbook images of that isolated stone city, built by the Incas more than 550 years ago, set my imagination on fire ☐. I had so many questions: Why was it built? Why was it abandoned? I convinced myself that I had to go there one day.

B That day finally came. Last year my fiancé and I spent a week in Peru, and all I can say is that Machu Picchu exceeded my expectations in every possible way. When I saw the Inca ruins for the first time, I was blown away ☐ by the perfection. Was it the giant stones, so well preserved? The extraordinary temples? Maybe the stunning ☐ views? It's hard to tell.

C Machu Picchu lies just fifty miles from Cusco, the starting point for any visit. It's an amazing city with colorful markets, fine restaurants, and gorgeous ☐ monuments. If you have a sweet tooth, check out the ChocoMuseo, where you'll eat the best chocolate in the country. Plus, it'll give you the energy you'll need to climb up the Inca trail. Once in Machu Picchu, don't miss the Temple of the Sun – it's truly awe-inspiring ☐.

D Machu Picchu is located nearly 2.5 kilometers above sea level, so it'll take your breath away ☐! Take it easy and drink plenty of water so your body can get used to the altitude. As a rule, the best time to visit Machu Picchu is between May and August, outside the rainy season. But, beware! Daily visitor numbers are strictly controlled, so be sure to book your trip way in advance.

E Machu Picchu is magnificent beyond your wildest dreams ☐. No wonder it's been named one of the New Seven Wonders of the World. I'm already looking forward to going back next year!

C Read *Write it right!* Then scan the report and write 1 or 2 next to the highlighted examples.

Write it right!

Two ways to make your description come alive are:

1 Avoid the word *nice*, and try not to overuse *beautiful*. Use more "colorful" synonyms:
The place was absolutely **breathtaking**.

2 Use figurative expressions:
It was a gorgeous beach spoiled by **a sea of tourists**.

D Read *Common mistakes*. Then correct six mistakes in the paragraph.

Common mistakes

The place was ~~very~~ *absolutely* stunning.

New York is one of the most multicultural ~~city of~~ *cities in* the world.

I'~~ve been in~~ *went to* Bangkok in 2010.

Don't use *very* with extreme adjectives, and be careful with plurals and tenses!

If you never went to Cartagena, located on Colombia's northern coast, you don't know what you're missing. It's a very gorgeous city and one of the most popular tourist attraction of the country. My favorite place is the Café del Mar, a great spot to watch the sunset over the old city walls. It's very amazing! I've been there last December and it was very crowded, so I suggest you go in October or November.

E **Your turn!** Describe the place you talked about in 11B. Write about 200 words.

Before
Organize your notes into five paragraphs to answer the questions from 11A.

While
Use colorful and figurative expressions from Lucy's report and *Write it right!* Check your grammar, too, for common mistakes.

After
Proofread carefully. Email your text to a classmate before sending it to your teacher.

Review 5

Units 9–10

1 Speaking

A Look at the photos on p.94.

1 Note down your impressions of the people using these expressions:

keep quiet mingle open up reveal small talk think out loud think over think up

2 In groups, share information. Who seems introverted? Who seems extroverted?

3 Take turns describing how you usually react in these situations.

At parties, I like to mingle and get to know new people.

Really? I hate small talk.

B Search "extrovert or introvert" and take a new personality quiz. Then share something new you learned about yourself.

I learned a new word. I'm an "ambivert." I really like to socialize, but I also like time by myself.

2 Listening

A R5.1 Listen to a conversation between Daisy and an employee of a car rental company. Number the problems in the order mentioned.

- [ ] The employee doesn't know much about the device.
- [ ] The only office is at the airport.
- [ ] Daisy can't hear a voice on the GPS.
- [ ] Refunds are only given through the website.
- [ ] The boss is away.
- [ ] The directions are wrong.

B **Make it personal** In pairs, discuss these questions.

1 Describe a specific travel problem that you've had. What happened in the end?

2 Was anyone able to help you?

Once I was locked in the bathroom of a hotel, and I couldn't get out ...

3 Grammar

A Eileen would like to take a study-abroad vacation. Change her questions to a program director to indirect questions, using the words in parentheses.

1 Are there any two-week Portuguese programs in Salvador Bahia? (Do you happen to know ...?)
2 Where do students stay? (Do you have any idea ...?)
3 How many hours a day are classes? (I wonder ...)
4 Is there a placement exam? (Could you tell me ...?)
5 What methodology does the teacher use? (I'd like to know ...)
6 Are there organized social activities? (Can you ask someone ...?)

B Make it personal Note down four indirect questions a visitor to your town or city might ask. In pairs, role play helping the "tourist."

C Complete Eileen's reactions to her vacation (1–5) with a form of *be used to* or *get used to*. Then combine the sentences using *which*.

1 In the beginning, I had some trouble *getting used to* the food. It was very spicy.
I had some trouble getting used to the food, which was very spicy.
2 I ______________ speaking Portuguese, either. It was overwhelming at first.
3 But it was easy to ______________ early morning classes. It was great because I had the rest of the day to sightsee.
4 I also ______________ singing in Portuguese every day because my teacher loved music. It was amazing.
5 And now I ______________ living with a family and speaking Portuguese at breakfast. It's such a great way to improve my language skills!

4 Writing

Write a paragraph about a problem you may encounter when you move abroad and offer a solution. Include at least four of these words or expressions.

in order to	while	although	as
so that	unlike	despite	due to

5 Self-test

Correct the two mistakes in each sentence. Check your answers in Units 9 and 10. What's your score, 1–20?

1 I'd like to live by my own, but I might have trouble get used to the quiet.
2 I was claiming the truth, but the police thought I was making the story.
3 Students cheat on their exams will end being expelled.
4 People are always chew gum in class, that drives me up the wall.
5 If you raise a lot your voice, it doesn't make people see eye and eye with you.
6 I'm really looking forward my trip with an old friend of me.
7 You have to checkout by 11, so you'd better ask for a wakeup call.
8 I'd like to know did anyone call and where is the nearest bank.
9 I miss the bustle and hustle of city life, and I can't used to the country.
10 The view was awe-inspire and it took my breath.

6 Point of view

Choose a topic. Then support your opinion in 100–150 words, and record your answer. Ask a partner for feedback. How can you be more convincing?

a You think small talk is a total waste of time. OR
You think small talk is a good way to meet new people and feel comfortable with them.
b You think social injustice is the worst problem facing society. OR
You think a lack of respect for the environment is far worse.
c You think living abroad is something everyone should do. OR
You think living abroad is very difficult and not for everyone.
d You think a foreign accent is something people should try to get rid of. OR
You think a foreign accent is like a foreign culture and should be respected.

11 »

What recent news has caught your eye?

1 Listening

A 11.1 Listen and match news items 1–6 to photos a–f. Then decide the section each is from.

arts business local science sports style

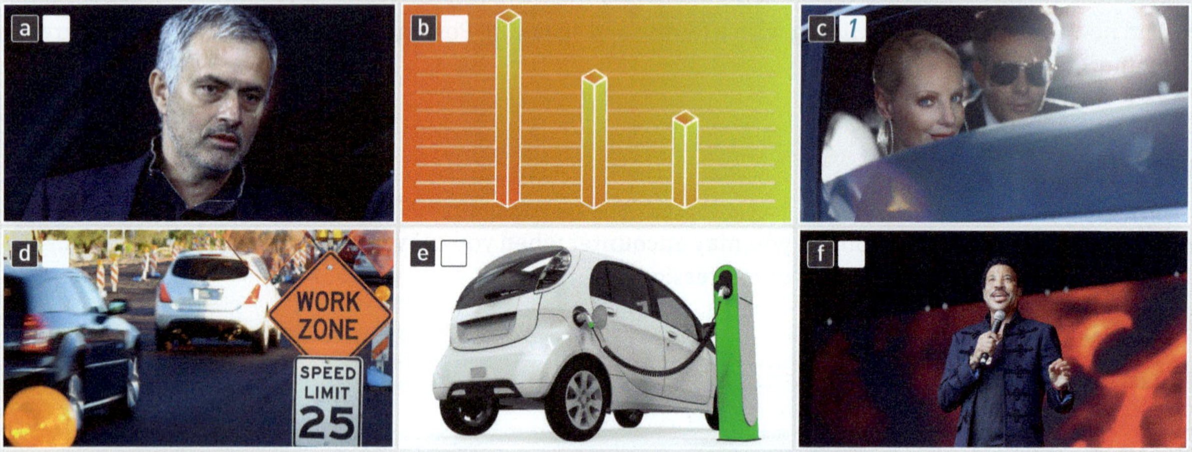

News story 1 must be the style section. That's where they talk about celebrity gossip.

Talking about the news

News is singular and uncountable.

I read **some** news that **was** shocking.
I'm interested in business **news** / **the** arts.
I enjoy reading **the** science **section**.

B 11.2 A reporter from A is doing a survey. Listen and note down Jack's answers in 1–3 words.

1 Favorite news topic?	
2 How often?	
3 In print or on digital media?	
4 Favorite news source?	
5 News alerts?	

C 11.2 Memory test! Try to complete 1–5. Listen again to check. Anything in common with Jack?

1 Jack follows the news so he won't seem ________ in front of his friends.
2 He is also interested in ________ , but he doesn't follow this area.
3 He only watches ________ when he's away from home.
4 He likes the ________ in his online magazine, but he would like to see more ________ and ________ .
5 He looks at his news feed on ________ and ________ .

Call me old-fashioned, but I still read a printed newspaper almost every day.

D **Make it personal** Choose a news story you've followed. In groups, share and ask follow-up questions. Any surprises?

Well, I'm studying politics, so I've been following the news story about ...

Oh, I didn't hear about that at all. When did it happen? ...

2 Vocabulary: The news

A 11.3 Circle the choice that is closest in meaning to the **highlighted** words. Listen to check.

1 I try to **keep up with** what's going on.
A stay informed
B tell people

2 It's such an **accurate** source of information.
A free from error and true
B with errors or not true

3 I wish they'd post more **behind-the-scenes** stuff.
A official
B usually hidden

4 They're **not biased** in favor or against any particular artist.
A neutral
B unfair

5 I tend to **skip** most stories.
A read in detail
B maybe glance at headlines, but not read

6 If a headline **catches my eye**, I click on the link.
A attracts my attention
B worries me

B Complete 1–5 with items from A. Then, in pairs, change the underlined words to make them true for you.

1 The evening news is usually __________, but not always. Sometimes they don't seem to check their facts .
2 I always try to __________ the latest news about sports.
3 Our main TV network is __________ against the government.
4 When presidents get together, it would be fascinating to know what actually happens __________ .
5 When I check the news, I __________ most of it and move straight to the horoscope section.

3 Pronunciation: Question intonation

A 11.4 Listen to and repeat the examples. Then check (✔) the correct rules.

1 Do you have a favorite news source?
2 What does that include?
3 Can I pick several topics or only one?

1 *Yes / No* questions usually have a ☐ rising ↗ ☐ falling ↘ intonation.
2 *Wh*-questions usually have a ☐ rising ☐ falling intonation.
3 Questions with *or* have a ☐ rising ☐ falling intonation on the first choice(s), but a ☐ rising ☐ falling intonation on the last one.

B 11.5 Listen to 1–5 and write a ↗, b ↘ or c ↗ ↘. Then listen again, copying the speaker's intonation.

1 __________ 2 __________ 3 __________ 4 __________ 5 __________

C Make it personal Give your opinions on the news!

1 Interview a new partner to complete the survey in 1B. Ask for lots of detail. Use words and expressions from 2A.

Common mistakes

Turn up the radio, I can't ~~listen to~~ hear the news.

OK. What's your favorite news topic?

Well, I really like to keep up with sports, but I usually skip the style section.

Do you mainly follow local teams or international ones?

2 Search for and read a news story about your city or country in a well-known English-language newspaper. Discuss 1–3.

1 Was it easy to understand, or were some parts difficult?
2 Was everything included, or were some important parts left out?
3 Overall, did the English version seem fair or biased?

4 Language in use

A 11.6 In the news, a "blooper" refers to a mistake made in public. Guess bloopers 1–3. Then listen and fill in the blanks. How close were you?

Some of our favorite news bloopers of all time
1
A reporter was doing a story on pets that act like humans when, suddenly, the dog he was holding ________ on live TV.
2
A news anchor ________ in the middle of a news story, before millions of viewers.
3
A TV network interviewed a woman, who they believed was an economist. However, she ________ .

B 11.6 Listen again. T (true) or F (false)?

1 The dog had been behaving strangely.
2 Viewers had no idea whether the reporter was OK.
3 The news anchor woke up by himself.
4 He made a joke about his mistake.
5 The candidate lost her temper during the interview.

C Write R (relaxed) or VN (very nervous) for the highlighted expressions. Which ones were you familiar with?

1 No one really knows why the dog lost it like that. The reporter himself **claimed** that everything had been going well behind the cameras.
2 He kept his cool, though, and **reassured** viewers that he was fine.
3 The news anchor was woken up by his colleague, who stayed calm and **reminded** him he was on live TV!
4 He was able to keep it together and simply denied that he had fallen asleep. Then he **admitted** he was just kidding, of course.
5 Instead of freaking out, the candidate **warned** them they'd made a mistake, then she calmly got up and left the studio!

D Make it personal In pairs, answer 1–4.

1 Which story did you like best?

> The last story was great. I would have totally lost it, but she really kept her cool.

2 Can you recall any "bloopers," either by famous people or in comedy?
3 Have you ever made a "blooper" of your own, or been caught on camera at the wrong moment? How did you react?
4 What kinds of things make you laugh? Have you ever laughed at the wrong time?

cartoons   Internet memes   animals doing silly things
comedy shows / funny movies   people falling   stand-up comedians

5 Grammar: Reporting what people say (1)

A Read the grammar box and check (✔) the correct rules 1–3.

Reported statements and questions

The news anchor said, "You're right, I'm exhausted. I went to bed late last night."	The news anchor **admitted** (to us) (that) he was exhausted. He **said** (that) he'd gone to bed late the night before.
She asked, "Can I have a day off?"	She **asked** her boss if she could have a day off.
The announcer asked, "What are you doing here?"	The candidate **explained** (to the announcer) what she was doing there.

In reported speech:
1 You often move one tense ☐ **back** ☐ **forward**.
2 You ☐ **can** ☐ **cannot** omit *that* after a reporting verb.
3 Pronouns, time, and place expressions often ☐ **change** ☐ **stay the same**.

Grammar expansion p.158

B Read *Reporting verbs and indirect objects*. Put the bold verbs in 4C and 5A in the chart.

Reporting verbs and indirect objects

Memorize which reporting verbs are followed by indirect objects!
*He **told me** he was tired.* *She **said** she was fine.* *He **explained (to us)** he was tired.*

Indirect object required	No indirect object or, for some verbs, optional
tell	*say*

C Report the dialogue between a news anchor (Andy) and co-host (Sam). Do you think Andy's right?

Sam: Did you really fall asleep?
Andy: Of course I didn't fall asleep! Erm ... Well, actually, I did.
Sam: Everyone is probably talking about you.
Andy: Really? Well, that doesn't worry me.
Sam: Erm... The video has already been posted online.
Andy: Yeah, but it will create a lot of positive buzz.
Sam: Hmm ... How can you be so sure?

1 Sam asked Andy ...
2 First he denied ... Then he admitted ...
3 Sam warned ...
4 Andy reassured ...
5 Sam reminded ...
6 Andy explained ...
7 Sam asked ...

Common mistakes

I asked him whether ~~he's~~ *he was* OK. He ~~explained / admitted / said me~~ *explained / admitted / said* that he was sick.

D Make it personal Choose a situation and think through 1–3 to prepare. Share your stories in groups. Anything in common?

1 What was the situation?
2 What questions did you ask? What was the response? Use a variety of reporting verbs.
3 What happened in the end?

I told my boyfriend that he needed to save money, but he didn't listen and ...

When was the last time you ...?
had a small / big disagreement
denied you'd done something
reminded someone of a promise
tried to get out of doing something boring
explained something again and again
were warned about something

6 Reading

A Read the title and questions 1–4, and imagine the answers. Then read the text and put the questions back into the interview. There is one extra question.

1 What kind of content do people tend to connect with?
2 Are there dangers involved in posting a video that goes viral?
3 Are there specific things I can do to make my video go viral?
4 Can viral videos be created? Or do they happen by chance?

How to make your video go viral

Of the many millions of videos posted online every day, why do some clips stand out from the crowd and go on to attract millions of viewers – sometimes in a matter of hours? Media experts Stacey Wright and Kevin Murray explain to our readers why some videos go viral.

"We've postponed the wedding until we come up with something we can do at the ceremony that will become a viral video."

Q: ______________________________?

Stacey: Basically, the latter. Having a video go viral is like winning the lottery. It's incredibly hard – though certainly not impossible – to achieve. For every success story out there, there are thousands of flops.

Kevin: Stacey's answer got me thinking about what our goal should be when we create a video. It's important to catch people by surprise. As a rule, I think we should try to leave them speechless. Whether our content will go viral is another story – it may or may not happen. But we shouldn't focus on that goal right from the beginning.

Q: ______________________________?

Stacey: People's brains are wired to pay close attention to anything that goes against their expectations. This means that a video that contains an unusual image, a bold statement, or some sort of unexpected turn of events tends to strike a chord with viewers, otherwise it may do nothing for them.

Kevin: The most shareable videos convey strong emotions. In a world obsessed with money and deadlines, people want to get in touch with their humanity. They want romance, entertainment, anger, and joy. They want to burst out laughing. They want to be moved to tears. So, the more intense a video is, the more likely it is to be passed along.

Q: ______________________________?

Stacey: The first thing most people do before they decide whether or not to watch a video is check how long it is, so the main thing is to keep it short and sweet. When your video is ready, cut it in half, and then cut it in half again. Keep in mind that you're creating content for the 140-character Twitter® generation – people with increasingly short attention spans.

Kevin: Recent evidence actually suggests nearly one fifth of your viewers will leave your video after ten seconds. By a minute in, nearly half will have clicked away, so you can't save the best for last, really. One more thing, people can be incredibly cruel online! You can't let their comments get to you.

B 11.7 Listen to check. Notice the /eɪn/ sound in the underlined words.

C Who made points 1–6? S (Stacey), K (Kevin), B (both), or N (neither)?

1 It's no use trying to make a video go viral.
2 People are interested in content that moves them.
3 People are interested in content that surprises them.
4 Twitter® is not a good platform for sharing videos.
5 You have to grab the viewer's attention from the beginning.
6 If your video goes viral, you can't be too sensitive.

D Make it personal In groups, answer 1–4. Similar opinions?

1 Who do you think made the best points, Stacey or Kevin?
2 Why else might a video go viral? Would you like one of yours to go viral? Why (not)?
3 How often do you leave a comment on a video? Do you tend to say mostly positive or negative things?
4 Have you ever posted a video yourself? Were you happy with the reaction?

7 Vocabulary: Emotional reactions

A 11.8 Review the highlighted expressions in 6A, then complete expressions 1–7 with the correct form of these verbs. There is one extra. Listen to check. Which expressions do you already use?

burst catch do get (two expressions) give leave move

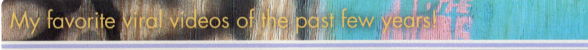

My favorite viral videos of the past few years!

Emotional baby This one will **(1)** _get_ you thinking, I'm sure. A ten-month-old baby gets teary-eyed as she watches her mother sing an old Rod Stewart song. This video **(2)** _____ me to tears when I first saw it, and it still **(3)** _____ to me whenever I play it again.

Sneezing baby panda A baby panda sneezes and the mother panda is **(4)** _____ by surprise. No big deal, right? Wrong. This clip is hilarious. When I first watched it, I **(5)** _____ out laughing so loud my family came running.

***Friday* by Rebecca Black** *Friday* is about a girl who's bored Monday through Thursday, but cheers up, well, guess when. When the video took off, people either loved or hated the clip. Nobody said, "It **(6)** _____ nothing for me." Did I like *Friday*? Well, let's just say it **(7)** _____ me speechless.

B In pairs, take turns miming and guessing the expressions in A (1–7) .

You're scratching your head. That must be "It gets you thinking."

C Make it personal Talk about viewing tastes!

1 In groups, search online for the videos in A. Vote for your favorite.
2 Share impressions of other clips you've seen. Use expressions in A. Any similar reactions?

music video movie sitcom episode soap opera amateur video documentary

What was the last documentary you watched?

I saw a terrifying one on forest fires a few weeks ago. It really left me speechless.

8 Language in use

HERE SHE COMES WITH THE ONE O'CLOCK NEWS

A Read the website. In pairs, answer 1–3.

1 What's the difference between gossip and news?
2 Which of the three types of gossip might the worker be? Which do you think is most common?
3 Rank the three gossip types most to least harmful.

Three types of gossip we've all met!

1 **The forwarder** Forwarders don't start rumors. They simply pass on gossip that comes to them.

2 **The seeker** Seekers are always on the lookout for gossip. They're always seeking someone to fill them in on the latest "news."

3 **The creator** Creators are the ones that start gossip and pass it on, even if they're not 100% sure.

Well, to me, the forwarder is the worst. If you just pass the news on, you're gossiping behind someone's back.

B 11.9 Listen to three conversations taking place in an office. Identify the gossip types.

1 ________ 2 ________ 3 ________

C 11.9 Listen again. M (the man), W (the woman), or N (neither)? Who do you think Truman is?

Who seems ...

Conversation 1	Conversation 2	Conversation 3
1 jealous of Lorrie?	3 to have trouble keeping a secret?	5 sure two people are dating?
2 to dislike gossip?	4 concerned about inconvenience?	6 most worried the rumor might spread?

D 11.10 Complete 1–4. Listen to check. Which expressions describe a) gossip? b) secrecy?

between you and me | my big mouth | keep it to myself | spread it around

1 I asked Truman for a raise last week, but he **refused** to even listen. By the way, this is ________, OK?
2 Truman **made** me swear I'd ________ .
3 If this leaks, Truman will kill me. Once he **threatened** to fire me because of ________ , remember?
4 I **begged** him not to ________ , and I'm sure he won't. Well, at least, I **expect** him not to.

E **Make it personal** Read the quotes. How strongly do you agree? Write ++ (strongly agree) to - - (strongly disagree). Then compare in groups. Which is the most controversial quote?

1 "I get accused all the time of having a big mouth. But if you ask me, guys gossip way more than girls do." (Meg Cabot)
2 "Whoever gossips to you will gossip about you." (Unknown / graffiti)
3 "Show me someone who never gossips, and I'll show you someone who isn't interested in people." (Barbara Walters)
4 "There is only one thing in the world worse than being talked about, and that is not being talked about." (Oscar Wilde)

Gender terms

Use *woman* and not *girl* to refer to someone who's not a child. Using "girl" can easily offend.

I disagree with the first one. My experience is that women find it harder than men to keep things to themselves.

Hmm ... I don't think gossip has anything to do with gender, actually. It has to do with personality.

9 Grammar: Reporting what people say (2)

A Read the grammar box. Then fill in the blanks with the bold verbs from 8D.

Reporting patterns with the infinitive and base form	
1 Verb + (not) + infinitive	She **agreed to tell** me a secret. I **promised to keep** it. Other verbs include ____________ and ____________ .
2 Verb + object + (not) + infinitive	I **persuaded him to reveal** what he knew. He **urged me not to spread** it around. Other verbs include ____________ and ____________ .
3 Verb + object + base form	I tried to talk about something else, but she didn't **let me change** the subject. ____________ follows the same pattern.

» Grammar expansion p.158

B Julia couldn't keep Truman's secret! Complete 1–6 using the verb given and a pattern from the grammar box. Then take turns reporting the whole conversation.

ANN: What were you two gossiping about?
JULIA: Erm ... Nothing.
ANN: (1) I'll keep it to myself. I promise!
JULIA: We weren't gossiping.
ANN: Well, I heard Truman's name. And Lorrie's.
JULIA: Hmm ... (2) I can't tell you. Sorry.
ANN: It must be something big. (3) Don't leave me in suspense!
JULIA: (4) Promise you won't say a word.
ANN: I swear.
JULIA: (5) I'll unfriend you on Facebook® if you do!
ANN: You have my word.
JULIA: (6) All right. I'll tell you.

1 Ann promised *to keep it to herself.*
2 Julia refused ...
3 Ann begged ...
4 Julia made ...
5 Then she threatened ...
6 She finally agreed ...

Ann asked Julia what she and her friend had been gossiping about.

C Make it personal Gossip!

1 ▶ 11.11 **How to say it** Complete the chart. Then listen, check, and repeat.

Common mistake

He made me ~~to~~ promise to keep it to myself.

	Gossiping	
	What they said	What they meant
1	You'll never ______ (who I ran into at the mall).	You have no idea (who ...)
2	My ______ are sealed. I won't tell a ______ .	I won't tell anyone.
3	Promise you'll ______ it between the two of us.	Promise you won't tell anyone.
4	You have my ______ .	I promise.

2 Choose a situation, imagine the details, and tell a partner. Ask him / her to be discreet! Use *How to say it* expressions.

You've won a small fortune on the lottery.
Someone in class is actually a secret agent.
You're dating a celebrity.
You've discovered a secret about a classmate.

3 Form new pairs and spread the news. Use reporting verbs. Who's the best gossip?

You'll never guess in a million years who I ran into at the mall over the weekend!

11.5 Would you enjoy being world-famous?

10 Listening

A 11.12 Listen to Rita Sycamore, a young actress, complaining to her friend, Jeb, about a news story. Note down three facts that were wrong.

B 11.13 Listen to the rest of the conversation. Check (✔) the correct answers.

1 Rita is bothered most by the ...
- ☐ invasion of her privacy.
- ☐ inaccuracies in the story.

2 Jeb's main point is that ...
- ☐ fame has more advantages than disadvantages.
- ☐ fame comes at a price.

C 11.13 Listen again and try to complete the sentences. Then check your answers against the definitions. Did you catch all the words and expressions?

1 You'll be ________________ for a day or two. And you know what they say, "Bad publicity is always better than no publicity."

2 Well, if you ask me, celebrity gossip is as ________________ as other more "serious" topics.

3 When you're a celebrity, there's no such thing as privacy. You're ________________ 24/7, and that's exactly the way it should be.

4 I think newspapers are ________________ to publish whatever they like.

entitle (v) (often passive): give someone a legal right or just a claim to receive or do something

in the spotlight (idiom): receiving public notice or attention

newsworthy (adj): important or interesting enough to report as news

the talk of the town (idiom): someone or something everyone is talking about

D Make it personal Choose a statement 1–4 in **C** you (dis)agree with, and share your opinions in pairs. Any major differences?

> I don't agree with the last one. Newspapers should try to be selective about what they publish.

11 Keep talking

A Check (✔) the problems you've experienced for 1–4. Then add one more problem to each group.

1 A TV channel you watch ...
- ☐ presents news that's biased or inaccurate.
- ☐ shows endless reruns of sitcoms.
- ☐ shows content inappropriate for children.

2 Your phone, cable, or Internet company ...
- ☐ keeps sending wrong bills.
- ☐ has terrible customer service.
- ☐ has lots of coverage and stability problems.

3 A recent documentary or news story about your country ...
- ☐ had wrong factual details.
- ☐ made too many generalizations.
- ☐ exaggerated small problems.

4 Your favorite online store ...
- ☐ makes it difficult to find what you want.
- ☐ has security problems.
- ☐ doesn't give enough product information.

B In groups, compare your ideas. Add more details and examples. Which are the most common complaints?

> WEID seems really biased. They only present one side of a story!

> Yeah, I know what you mean. The news just isn't accurate these days.

Common mistakes

There's too ~~many~~ *much* violence on TV.

There's not ^ *enough* educational content ~~enough~~.

12 Writing: A letter of complaint

A Read Rita's letter to the editor of an online newspaper. Which wrong fact from 10A is not mentioned?

Rita Sycamore
101 Maryland Avenue
Pittsburgh, PA 15212

Mr. Jerome Sacks
ID News and Views

May 23, 2016

Dear Mr. Sacks:

I am writing in regard to the photo and the article published in the entertainment section of your home page this morning ("TV star Rita Sycamore spotted with new boyfriend"). I happen to be the woman in the photo and I would like to call your attention to a number of inaccuracies in your article.

You claimed that the man in the photo was my new boyfriend, when, in reality, he is my vocal coach, and our relationship is strictly professional. To make matters worse, my age was incorrect, which shows a lack of attention to detail.

Above all, I am very surprised that a reputable newspaper like yours would even consider publishing stories like this one. It is my belief that celebrities are entitled to the same level of privacy as the general public.

I would like to ask you to remove the photo and article from your website in the next few hours. Tomorrow I will check to confirm that these steps have been taken. Thank you very much for your attention to this matter.

Sincerely,

Rita Sycamore

Rita Sycamore

B Circle the correct options.

A well-organized complaint letter presents the [**situation / solution**] in paragraph 1. It then moves on to a [**problem / suggestion**] in paragraph 2. In paragraph 3, it sometimes presents [**an opinion / only facts**]. Finally, in the last paragraph, the letter often [**makes a request / only gives a summary**].

C Read *Write it right!* Then write the more formal highlighted expressions 1–5 in the chart.

Write it right!

In a formal email or letter:

1. Begin your email with *Dear* + full name or *Dear Sir / Madam*. Sign off with *Sincerely (yours)*.
2. Put a colon (:) after the full name when you begin, but a comma (,) when you sign off.
3. Avoid contractions: ~~*I'm*~~ ***I am*** *writing to complain about ...*
4. Avoid informal language: *There were* ~~*lots of*~~ ***a number of*** (more formal) *inaccuracies in the article.*

"Well, actually ..."	1 ______
"about ..."	2 ______
"I think ..."	3 ______
"I want to point out ..."	4 ______
"Another problem is ..."	5 ______

D Complete 1–5, from different letters and emails, using formal expressions from C.

1. I am writing ______ the programming on your channel.
2. While you claim to have excellent customer service, ______, I had to call five times before someone could help me.
3. ______ the fact that there were a number of factual errors in your recent documentary.
4. ______ that there should be fewer stories on urban violence, especially in that time slot.
5. Your online store is not only hard to navigate. ______, it often lacks sufficient product information.

E **Your turn!** Write a 180-word letter or email complaining about a problem from 11A.

Before
Check the guidelines in B, and decide the main points you will make in each paragraph.

While
Re-read *Write it right!* Use at least four expressions from C, and check the level of formality.

After
Proofread your work carefully. Show it to another student before sending it to your teacher.

12 »

How optimistic are you?

1 Listening

A ▶ 12.1 Complete the quotes from a radio show with *an optimist* or *a pessimist*. Listen to check. Which is your favorite?

1 "I used to be __________, but now I know nothing is going to turn out as I expect." Sandra Bullock

2 "__________ sees the difficulty in every opportunity; __________ sees the opportunity in every difficulty." Winston Churchill

3 "The man who is __________ before 48 knows too much; if he is __________ after it, he knows too little." Mark Twain

Common mistakes

Overall, I'd say I'm ~~optimist~~ *an optimist*, but I'm a bit ~~pessimist~~ *pessimistic* about the interview.

Optimist and *pessimist* are nouns. *Optimistic* and *pessimistic* are adjectives.

B ▶ 12.2 Listen to the radio show survey and circle the correct answers. Do you feel the same way?

Are we becoming a city of pessimists?

Take the survey to help us find out!

How optimistic are you about ...?

☺ optimistic
😐 not sure
☹ pessimistic

1 your final exams ☺ / 😐 / ☹

2 your (future) career ☺ / 😐 / ☹

3 your team's chances ☺ / 😐 / ☹

4 this country's economy ☺ / 😐 / ☹

C ▶ 12.3 Complete the highlighted expressions in 1–4, using your intuition. Listen to check. Do you have similar ones in your language?

feet	fingers	proportion	store	tunnel	world

1 I keep telling myself that it's **not the end of the __________** (= not a tragedy) if I fail an exam or two, but deep down, I know I'll be really upset. Anyway, I'm **keeping my __________ crossed** (= hoping for the best).

2 They're going through a rough time right now, so who knows **what the future has in __________** (= what will happen) for me.

3 I know we've lost all the games so far this season, but now with this new coach, there might be **a light at the end of the __________** (= some hope).

4 The media tends to **blow things out of __________** (= exaggerate), but, on the whole, I think we're doing OK. Anyway, I try to **keep my __________ on the ground** (= be practical and sensible).

D In groups, take turns miming and guessing the expressions in **C**. Then remember all you can of each conversation. Check in **AS** 12.2 on p.164. Anything you missed?

E **Make it personal** In pairs, answer 1–4. Any surprises?

1 Take the survey in **B**. Use expressions from **C** in your answers.
2 Create two other questions to ask each other. Who's more optimistic?
3 Who's the most / least optimistic person in your family? How well do you get along?
4 Does the weather affect your general feelings of optimism / pessimism?

I love cold, rainy days, you know. The grayer the better! I feel really good.

Really? Rainy days always get me down.

2 Listening

A ▶ 12.4 Listen to three conversations. Are the people O (optimistic) or P (pessimistic)? Have you ever had a similar experience?

Conversation 1	Conversation 2	Conversation 3
1 Ed ______	3 Peter ______	5 Tom ______
2 Sonia ______	4 Kate ______	6 Linda ______

B ▶ 12.4 Listen again and check (✔) what you can infer about each person.

1 Ed wasn't surprised he got fired.
2 Sonia thinks Ed's age might have been a problem in the past.
3 Kate likes expensive cars.
4 Kate probably had a big car before.
5 Linda doesn't mind packing.
6 Linda has probably been to Paris before.

C **Make it personal** Take turns role playing an optimist / pessimist.

1 ▶ 12.5 **How to say it** Complete the chart. Listen, check, and repeat, copying the intonation.

Optimism and pessimism

	What they said	What they meant
1	Let's hope for the ______ .	Let's hope things will turn out well.
2	No ______ is good news.	
3	Look on the ______ side.	Try to find something good about this situation.
4	Better safe than ______ .	It's better to be cautious so you don't regret it later.
5	Yeah, ______ on! (informal)	What you want probably won't happen.
6	That's wishful ______ .	What you want is not realistic.

2 Choose two situations and role play them with a partner. Use *How to say it* expressions.

A ☹ You've just failed an important test. You think you might have to take the course again.
B ☺ Convince **A** that taking the course again will be a good idea.

A ☺ You've just inherited $1 million. You want to quit your job, invest the money, and live off the interest.
B ☹ You think quitting a steady job is too risky.

A ☺ You love to live dangerously. You want to go mountain climbing next weekend.
B ☹ You're scared of extreme sports. Remind **A** of all the risks involved.

3 Language in use

A 12.6 Listen to part 1 of an online program and match conversations 1–4 to pictures a–d. Label the items.

DYING TECHNOLOGIES: WHAT WE SAY ABOUT WHAT THE EXPERTS SAY

a ☐ ______

"Wireless chargers for smartphones are already on the market, and the possibility of Power WiFi is not that far off."
Yes, definitely. Soon you won't have to shout "Watch out! You're going to trip over that thing!" anymore. But we're talking [1] ______ years from now, at least.

b ☐ ______

"Very soon, people are going to be driving into a gas station for a recharge. Or maybe to fill up the tank with a clean [2] ______ , like ethanol."
Gas is bound to be replaced **by** ☐ greener fuels, but the combustion engine won't be going anywhere until electric cars become less [3] ______ .

c ☐ ______

"In the past few years, subscriptions have dropped **by** ☐ more than 50%. By the end of the decade, we'll be using [4] ______ only."
Yes, this trend is likely to continue, except in more remote areas, where there are relatively few cell phone [5] ______ .

ALL NEWSPAPERS
NOW ON MEMORY STICK
USB

d ☐ ______

"**By** ☐ 2020, printed newspapers and magazines will have disappeared without a trace. Online subscriptions are much cheaper."
Newsstands are still going to be around for a while. They'll attract new customers **by** ☐ selling [6] ______ and lottery tickets, for example.

B 12.7 Read the infographic in A and predict the missing information. Listen to part 2 to check. Did you guess correctly? Any you disagreed with?

> I'm not so sure about the first one. I think it will take ... years.

C Read *Uses of by*. Then write 1–4 next to the bold words in A.

Uses of *by*

By is the 30th most common word in English. Here are four important uses:

1 Expresses "not later than":
*I'll get back to you **by** Monday.*

2 Answers the question *how*:
*We're going **by** car.*

3 Indicates the amount:
*Prices have increased **by** 20%.*

4 Identifies the "doer" in passive sentences:
*The telephone was invented **by** Bell.*

D Make it personal In pairs, answer 1–4. Similar opinions?

> I think watches are totally useless. I know what time it is by looking at my phone.

1 Order the technologies in A in the order you think they will disappear.
2 Will you miss them? Why (not)?
3 Which other everyday items / jobs / activities would you like to disappear?
4 What do you think they should be replaced by?

doing dishes   ironing   plastic bags   postal workers   watches

4 Grammar: Talking about the future (1)

A Read the grammar box and write the correct numbers (1–3) next to the examples. Then find four more examples of 1 and 2 in the infographic.

Predictions with *going to*, *will*, future perfect, and future continuous

☐ TV sets **will / are going to become** increasingly rare.
☐ People **will / are going to be riding** driverless cars.
☐ Bookstores **will have disappeared** by 2030.

1 Actions completed before some point in the future.
2 Actions in progress at some point in the future.
3 Future predictions in general.

Will and *going to* are often interchangeable, but *going to* is more common when you are sure of your prediction because there is evidence:
*Watch out! You'**re going to spill** coffee on your phone.*

Common mistake

By the end of this lesson, you ~~will read~~ *will have read* 129 pages of *Identities 1*.

» Grammar expansion p.160

B More predictions! Correct four mistakes in the predictions below. There may be more than one answer.

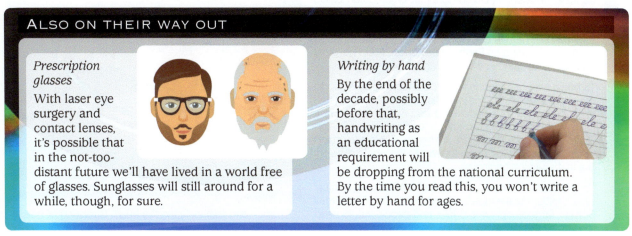

ALSO ON THEIR WAY OUT

Prescription glasses
With laser eye surgery and contact lenses, it's possible that in the not-too-distant future we'll have lived in a world free of glasses. Sunglasses will still around for a while, though, for sure.

Writing by hand
By the end of the decade, possibly before that, handwriting as an educational requirement will be dropping from the national curriculum. By the time you read this, you won't write a letter by hand for ages.

C Read *Other ways to make predictions*. Rephrase three sentences in **B** using *be likely to* and *be bound to*.

Other ways to make predictions

You can use *be (un)likely to* and *be bound to* when making predictions. *Be bound to* is more definite:
Next year **is likely to be** better than this year. (I'm pretty sure it will be better.)
Climate change **is bound to get** worse. (I'm almost certain it will get worse.)

D Make it personal In groups, guess what life will be like in 2050. Who predicts the brightest future?

English   food   household chores   marriage   post offices   school tests   shopping

I think ... are going to ...

... are bound to ...

By ... I think ... will have ...

... will be ... -*ing*

What do you think the future has in store for us as far as household chores are concerned?

I'm sure people won't be spending their free time vacuuming or ironing.

5 Reading

A In groups, make a list of things you know about Mars in one minute. Which group has the longest list?

> Scientists have found water on Mars, right? But I'm not sure whether it's drinkable.

Common mistake

I don't believe there's intelligent life ~~in~~ *on* other planets.

B In pairs, discuss the photo. Ask *where, what, who, when, why*? Read paragraph 1 to check. Does the writer feel optimistic or pessimistic about the project?

C Read only the first sentence of paragraph 2 and guess why the writer feels this way. Then read to check. Do the same for paragraphs 3–5. Were you surprised?

Not the kind of place to raise your kids. Or is it?

After the blockbuster movie *The Martian* in 2015, it seems we've been witnessing a new wave of enthusiasm for the idea that in the near future, some of us are going to be living on Mars. A Dutch nonprofit organization called Mars One, for example, is hoping to send four people on a one-way trip to Mars by 2026, as the beginning of a permanent human colony, which could in the long run ease overcrowding on Earth. To be honest, I still [1] **have my doubts** about whether this is a viable mission.

To begin with, getting there will be a nightmare. A trip to Mars will take up to nine months, which is a long time, especially when four people will be floating around in a tiny capsule, subjected to low gravity and insanely high levels of radiation. Then there are the inevitable equipment failures, which could [2] **pose a threat** to the whole mission. But that's just the beginning.

People seem to [3] **overlook the fact that** Mars is horribly inhospitable. The average temperature is minus 63 degrees Celsius, far too cold for it to rain, and people would need to [4] **figure out a way** to endure the year-long cold. Then there's breathing. The atmosphere is 96% carbon dioxide, so oxygen must be artificially synthesized, which will be [5] **hard to pull off**. And extremely dangerous, since peaks of oxygen may be potentially lethal, too.

Another key question is how the crew's health will be affected. Their bones and muscles evolved under Earth's gravity and on Mars they will weigh 30% of what they weigh on Earth. This means they're bound to lose a lot of muscle mass – and that includes the heart. Speaking of heart, their feelings of isolation and loneliness will probably be devastating, especially as time goes on. We don't [6] **have a clue** how this will affect their mental health.

And finally, the costs are going to be quite literally astronomical. At an estimated cost of $6 billion (!) for the first flight, the whole project begs the question: Is colonizing Mars worth the investment – and the risk? Wouldn't it be wiser to use this money to fix our own planet first?

D Read *How to know if a writer is certain*. Then re-read the article and write + (more certain) or – (less certain) for 1–5, according to the text. Underline the evidence.

1 There will be technical problems in the spacecraft.
2 Too much oxygen will kill them.
3 Their hearts will get weaker.
4 They will go crazy eventually.
5 The mission will cost $6 billion.

How to know if a writer is certain

	more certain	less certain
adverbs	The whole thing will **inevitably** fail.	It will cost $10 million, **possibly** $20 million.
adjectives	It's **bound** to go wrong.	There are a lot of **potential** problems.
expressions	It's off to a bad start, **without a doubt**.	**Who knows** what's in store for us.
modals	It'**ll** be a disaster.	It **might** backfire eventually.

E 12.8 Read and listen. Notice the schwa /ə/ in the words ending in *-al* and *-able*.

F Make it personal In pairs, answer 1–3. Anything in common?

1 Why would anyone volunteer for a mission like that? Would you?
2 How would you answer the last question in paragraph 5? Give three reasons.
3 Imagine you're one of the astronauts. You can take three personal objects with you. What would you take and why? (Remember: No phones!)

I think I'd take a photo of my family.

You mean, so you could feel close to them, even if you couldn't see them?

6 Vocabulary: Expressions for discussing innovation

A Match the bold words 1–6 in the article in 5C with their meanings a–f. Then in pairs, test each other. Say the highlighted expression from memory and give an example sentence.

a ☐ achieve c 1 feelings of uncertainty e ☐ find
b ☐ ignore d ☐ relevant information f ☐ represent

Doubts ...

Have my doubts. I have my doubts about life on Mars.

B Complete the forum entries with the highlighted expressions 1–6 in 5C. Who do you agree with?

Cars that drive themselves: a blessing or a curse?

Aron4: The problem with the scientists behind this new driverless car is that they tend to [1] ____________ a lot of people actually enjoy driving – at least I know I do. So I [2] ____________ about whether self-driving cars will ever become popular.

Paula87: As far as the technology itself is concerned, I imagine a self-driving car wouldn't be [3] ____________ . In fact, lots of prototypes already exist and have been tested on roads, with very few accidents, which means they probably won't [4] ____________ to pedestrians and other drivers.

JJWilcox: Everyone's hyped up about driverless cars, but the truth is, we don't [5] ____________ what our roads will be like with thousands of these. How safe and reliable are these cars, really?

Freerider©: Another car? Really? What the government should do is [6] ____________ to persuade people to use their bikes or public transportation.

C Make it personal Rate each innovation below from 1 (unnecessary) to 4 (very necessary). In groups, share your ideas. Which innovation is most (least) popular?

Innovations we might see by 2025:

the end of physical classrooms DNA mapping at birth to manage disease risk pills to replace sleep
4D TVs cosmetic face transplants the end of baldness music written by machines

I gave "music written by machines" a 2.

Me too. Machines are bound to be less creative than people!

7 Language in use

A In groups, make a list of excuses people usually make in situations 1–3. Which cartoon do you like best?

1 Leaving work early

2 Traffic violations

3 Being late

When people want to leave work early, they often say, "I'm not feeling well."

B 12.9 Listen to Don's excuses and take notes. Who do you think believed him?

	2:00 p.m.	3:00 p.m.	4:00 p.m.
1 Who's he talking to?			
2 What's the excuse?			
3 Why did he make it?			

C 12.10 Complete the text with the words from the mind map. Listen to Don's conversation the next day to check.

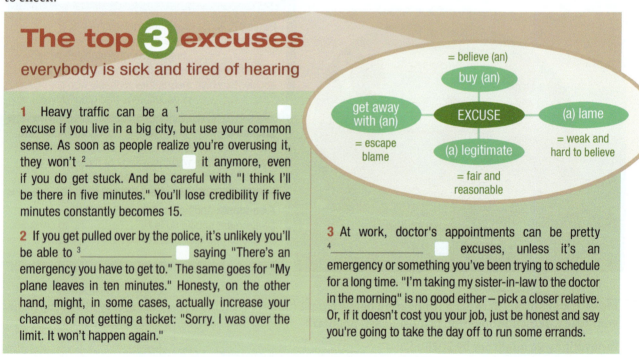

The top 3 excuses
everybody is sick and tired of hearing

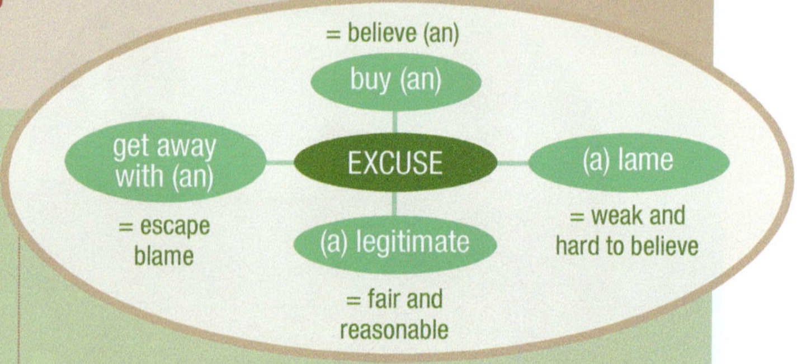

1 Heavy traffic can be a [1] ___________ excuse if you live in a big city, but use your common sense. As soon as people realize you're overusing it, they won't [2] ___________ it anymore, even if you do get stuck. And be careful with "I think I'll be there in five minutes." You'll lose credibility if five minutes constantly becomes 15.

2 If you get pulled over by the police, it's unlikely you'll be able to [3] ___________ saying "There's an emergency you have to get to." The same goes for "My plane leaves in ten minutes." Honesty, on the other hand, might, in some cases, actually increase your chances of not getting a ticket: "Sorry. I was over the limit. It won't happen again."

3 At work, doctor's appointments can be pretty [4] ___________ excuses, unless it's an emergency or something you've been trying to schedule for a long time. "I'm taking my sister-in-law to the doctor in the morning" is no good either – pick a closer relative. Or, if it doesn't cost you your job, just be honest and say you're going to take the day off to run some errands.

D **Make it personal** In pairs, talk about the last lame excuse you or someone else made. Did you / the other person buy it?

Last week my oldest friend forgot to call me on my birthday and said her phone was stolen. Of course I didn't buy it. I mean, she could have Skyped me.

Pretty lame, huh? Or at least sent an e-card or message!

8 Grammar: Talking about the future (2)

A Study the examples and complete rules a–d with 1–4. Then write the correct rule (a–d) next to the quotes in 7C.

Expressing plans and intentions, decisions, and scheduled events

Listen, I have to go. The bus **leaves** at seven.
I'**m going to join** a gym. I'**m signing up** today!

My battery is almost dead. I'**ll give** you a call later!
I'm not sure, but maybe I'**ll take** a course this summer.

Use the ... 1 simple present 2 present continuous as future 3 future with *going to* 4 future with *will*

a ☐ for a decision or promise you make at the moment you're speaking.
b ☐ for events on a schedule or timetable, with verbs like *open*, *close*, *arrive*, and *start*.
c ☐ for plans and intentions you're not sure of with expressions like *I guess*, *I think*, and *probably*.
d ☐ or ☐ for a fixed decision or plan you've already made.

Grammar expansion p.160

B ▶ 12.11 Don's boss, Miranda, is having a difficult day at the office. Circle the best answers 1–6. Listen to check.

1 I [**'ll fire** / **'m going to fire**] Sue Ann. She's been late every day for two weeks!
2 Please talk to her first. Or I [**'ll talk** / **'m talking**] to her for you.
3 OK, I [**give** / **'ll give**] her one more chance. But this is the last one!
4 Excuse me, Miranda, I [**'ll probably be** / **'m probably being**] late tomorrow.
5 I [**'m taking** / **'ll take**] my grandmother to the doctor.
6 Unacceptable! Our meeting [**starts** / **will start**] at 9:00 a.m.! One more excuse and you're fired!

C Read *Time clauses*. Then complete 1–4 with a suitable verb.

Time clauses

Always use the simple present in time clauses with words like *when*, *after*, *as soon as*, *before*, and *until*:

I'm going to buy a car **as soon as** I turn 18. (= immediately after)
I'm finishing the report **before** I leave.
I won't leave **until** the rain stops. (= up to the point that)

Common mistake

I think she'll get promoted as soon as she ~~will graduate~~ graduates.

1 Going abroad: "I'm not going abroad until my English ________ better."
2 Saving money: "I'm going to start saving money when my boss ________ me a raise."
3 Finishing an assignment: "I'll get started after I ________ the dishes and check my newsfeed."
4 Eating healthier food: "I'll change my diet when my doctor ________ I'm in trouble."

D Rewrite 1–4 in C using the words below. Which sentence is true for you?

1 as soon as 2 until 3 before 4 until

I'm going abroad as soon as my English is better.

E Make it personal In pairs, share stories about 1–3. Make one untrue. Can your partner guess which one?

1 Something you're not going to do even though you should. What's your excuse?
2 Someone you're meeting in the next few days even though you'd rather not. If you make an excuse, will he/she buy it?
3 Something old / useless you think you'll throw away soon. What's wrong with it?

I think I'll throw away all of my CDs this week. They take up a lot of space.

Me too. I'm getting rid of mine as soon as I can upload all of them.

9 Listening

A 12.12 Listen to Fred talking about a contest he entered. Answer 1–3.

1 What does Fred have to do?
2 What was the example he gave Tina?
3 How much older is Fred in photo 2?

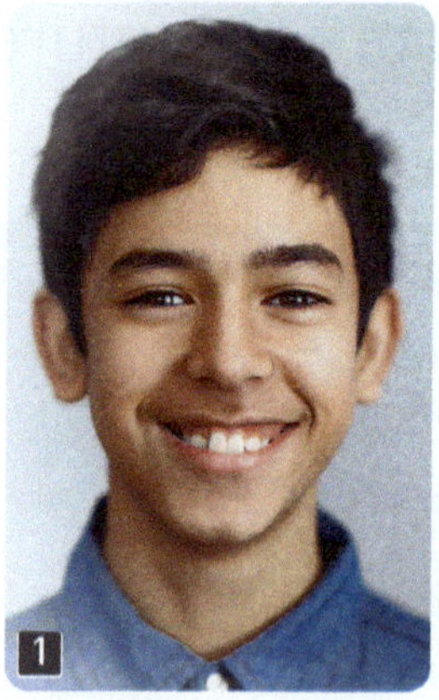
1

2

B 12.13 Listen to Fred 10 years later and complete sentences 1–4. One choice is used twice. Is Fred pleased with his decisions?

a expected to   b didn't expect to   c wondered if he'd

When Fred was younger, he ...

1 ______ look this old.
2 ______ become a teacher.
3 ______ have a girlfriend.
4 ______ live at home after graduation.

C 12.12 & 12.13 Complete 1–7 with the correct prepositions. Listen again to check. Did you understand all the highlighted expressions?

1 I'm taking part ______ a writing contest.
2 I could do ______ a little extra cash.
3 What ______ earth is that?
4 You could start with something ______ the lines of "Dear Tina ..."
5 Well, it's now a number of years ______ the road.
6 It may not satisfy me totally ______ a personal level.
7 That should be the least ______ your problems.

10 Keep talking

A Think ahead 10 years. What would you say now to your future self? Make notes on at least three topics.

career   family life   fitness and health   friends   looks   love life   money   studies   travel

I'm pretty sure you'll ...
I'm assuming ...
I'd love to ...
I hope you won't ...
I wonder ...

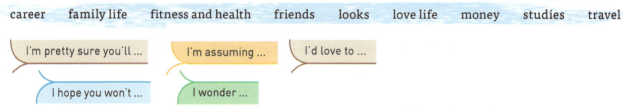

B In groups, compare ideas about your future selves. Any coincidences?

What do you think your life will be like in 10 years?
Well, I'm assuming I will have started my own business by then.
Really? What kind of business?

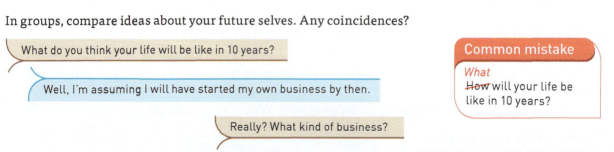

Common mistake

~~How~~ *What* will your life be like in 10 years?

11 Writing: An email to your future self

A Read Nina's email to her future self. Are any of your ideas from 10A mentioned?

From: **Present Nina**
Subject: **Future Me**
To: **Future Nina**

Dear Future Me,

I've just come across a website that allows someone to send an email to his or her "future self" 10 years from now. I thought, "What a cool idea!" And so, here it is: my first email to you, "Future Me." Today is August 30, 2016, so, when you read this, [1]you'll be celebrating your 27th birthday. I know you're not too crazy about birthday parties, so I hope you make it through this one! Well, at least you'll be surrounded by all the people you love, that's for sure.

Next year you're going off to college. Or maybe you'll end up taking a year off to travel around the world and do some volunteer work. Who knows? By 2022, [2]you'll have graduated and found a nice job in your field. Aren't you lucky that, unlike some of your classmates, you'll be able to build a career from your passion – looking after animals? Call me an optimist, but I'm sure [3]you'll become one of the best vets in the city!

As to marriage ... Well, I could be wrong, of course, but I have my doubts you'll want to settle down and have kids before you're in your thirties. You've always valued your freedom more than anything else and something tells me you'll want to enjoy your single life for as long as you can. Hmm ... What else? Oh, that trip to Cappadocia, Turkey, to go hot-air ballooning? When you read this email again, [4]you'll have done that – maybe more than once! Trust me!

Aren't you proud of yourself for writing this email in English? Wow! [5]You'll be an advanced student next year! Doesn't time fly? You may be a bit tired of studying English right now, but stick with it! I'm sure it will have been worthwhile in the end.

Future Nina, you'll have a bright future, wherever you are and whatever you may be doing. I'll do my best to help, I promise.

Love,
Present Nina

B In pairs, explain the purpose of each paragraph.

I think the first one explains what the email is about.

Yes, and it tells us something about Nina. It's an introduction.

C Read *Write it right!* Then complete rules 1–2 with *after* or *before*.

Write it right!

Use adverbs for emphasis and to show how certain you are of something:

I hope that, by the end of the year, my boss will have **finally** promoted me to assistant manager. I'll **definitely** be making more money, I know, but my workload will **inevitably** increase, too.

In sentences with *will*, adverbs usually go ...

1 ________ *will* and ________ the main verb.
2 ________ the auxiliary *be*, but ________ the auxiliary *have*.

D Add these adverbs to the underlined phrases in A (1–5).

1 (probably) *you'll probably be celebrating*
2 (hopefully) ________
3 (eventually) ________
4 (certainly) ________
5 (officially) ________

E **Your turn!** Write an email of 200–250 words to your future self.

Before
Choose three or four topics from *Keep talking* in 10A.

While
Refer to B and make sure each paragraph has a clear purpose. Re-read *Write it right!* and use a variety of adverbs in your predictions.

After
Post your writing, and if possible, set a delivery date to receive your own email.

Review 6

Units 11–12

1 Listening

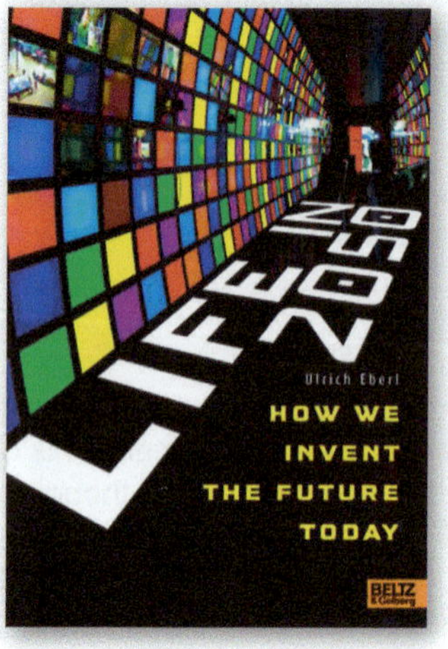

A R6.1 Listen to a conversation about Ulrich Eberl's book *Life in 2050*. Complete the sentences.

By 2050 ...

1 you'll be using a computer the size of a ______________ .
2 a computer will be able to ______________ a car.
3 there will be ______________ farms in cities.
4 cars will be ______________ to each other.
5 a "smart apartment" will recognize your ______________ .
6 one in every six people will be over the age of ______________ .

B **Make it personal** In groups, suggest as many innovations as you can for 2050 in two minutes. Which group has the most interesting ones?

I think food production will have doubled by 2050.

We'll be eating a lot more ...

2 Grammar

A Report the conversation using the words in parentheses.

GINA: I have something to tell you. (Gina told Len ...)

Gina told Len that she had something to tell him.

LEN: Really? Is it good news? (Len asked Gina ...)
GINA: Not really. (Gina admitted ...) I fell asleep during my interview last week. (She explained ...)
LEN: I don't believe it! (Len said ...)
GINA: It's true. (Gina assured Len ...) I don't think I got the job. (She added ...)
LEN: It's unlikely. (Len warned Gina ...) But some bosses have a kind heart! (But he reminded her ...)

B Report what happened next using the words in parentheses.

1 "Call your interviewer in the morning." (Len urged Gina ...)
2 "Please give me another chance." (Gina begged her interviewer ...)
3 "I'll go to bed early from now on." (She promised ...)
4 "I can't schedule another interview." (First, her interviewer refused ...)
5 "OK, I'll think it over and call you next week." (Then he agreed ...)

C Circle the correct future form for each of Gina's sentences.

1 [**I'm going to have / I'll have**] another interview tomorrow after all.
2 [**I'm getting / I get**] there early. That's for sure.
3 Maybe [**I'll go / I'm going**] to sleep at 9:00 p.m., too.
4 As soon as [**I'll get / I get**] home, I'll start preparing.

D **Make it personal** In pairs, role play one of these situations.

1 Report an embarrassing incident that happened to you or someone you know.
2 Apologize for something you've done and say what you've decided to do differently.

3 Reading

A Read the blog about the future. The main purpose of the blog is to ...

- [ ] frighten people.
- [ ] encourage people to read about environmental problems.
- [ ] encourage people to join the organization and take action.

FIFTY YEARS FROM NOW ... by David Montalbán

When most people think about the future, they only think of positive developments: advances in medicine and technology, better living conditions, higher salaries. Concernedcitizens.id. is more realistic. The future is in our hands only if we are aware and responsible. Some of these facts may shock you!

- In a recent year, 22 million people, many of them poor, were displaced by natural disasters. People living in coastal areas will continue to suffer in the years ahead. Yet, despite enormous evidence to the contrary, some scientists still argue that computer models are "not sophisticated enough" to predict climate change. Is it that they don't want to spend money to control carbon monoxide emissions that raise the earth's temperature? What can you do to prevent global warming?
- By 2050, the Earth's population will have increased from 7 billion to 9.6 billion people. There will not be enough resources for so many people, especially if flooding and drought increase due to climate change. We will need more recycling and more solar energy. Farmers will need incentives to grow food in an environmentally sound way. But do you know how to prevent overuse of fertilizers or how to increase sustainable farming on dry land? And do you recycle all you can?

If these and other facts concern you, become involved! Contact us at concernedcitizens.id to see how you can get help. The future is now!

B In pairs, search on "global warming" or "preserving our resources." Then answer one of the writer's questions in a way you think he'd agree with.

4 Self-test

Correct the two mistakes in each sentence. Check your answers in Units 11 and 12. What's your score, 1–20?

1 I try to keep up the news, even though it's often bias.
2 My girlfriend said me she was sorry and admitted me she was wrong.
3 I promised her to keep the secret, and I agreed her not to tell anyone.
4 I explained my teacher I'm not sure of the answer.
5 My mother persuaded me apologize and she made me to call right away.
6 I'm definitely optimist, so I'm keeping my fingers cross about the future.
7 We're going there on bus, and as soon as we'll arrive, I'll be in touch.
8 By the time you read this, you will almost finish *Identities*, and you will likely to know a lot of English!
9 I'm giving you a call later. Maybe I'm taking a nap first.
10 I visit Larry this weekend, so I won't see you until I'll get back.

5 Point of view

Choose a topic. Then support your opinion in 100–150 words, and record your answer. Ask a partner for feedback. How can you be more convincing?

a You think gossip is part of human nature and no big deal. OR
You think gossip can be very dangerous and should be avoided at all cost.

b You think the economic situation is bad, and there's a lot to be pessimistic about. OR
You think there will always be jobs for people who are well qualified, and it's important to be optimistic.

1 More on *so* do after 7.2

So vs. *such* as intensifiers		
I'm	**so**	excited about the concert.
It's going to be		great!
I'm	**such**	a fan of Bruno Mars.
He's		a great singer.
There are	**so many**	people out there.
I've never heard	**so much**	noise.
Use *so* + adjective, but use *such* + (adjective +) noun. Use *so many* + count nouns, but *so much* + non-count nouns.		

Expressing purpose with *so as (not) to*		
I left an hour early	**so as to**	be on time for the interview.
I gave up my seat	**so as not to**	seem selfish.
So as (not) to means "in order (not) to," but is more formal. The negative *so as not to* is more common in conversation than the affirmative *so as to*.		

2 *because*, *because of*, and *for* do after 7.2

I couldn't go to the concert	**because of**	the expense. rain.
	because	it was expensive. I didn't have an umbrella.
John was fired	**for**	arguing with his boss.

More on *for*	
To express a reason	*For* meaning "because" or "as a result of" can replace *because of* in very few situations. Memorize phrases with *for* when you hear them. ▶ I canceled my trip **for (because of)** health reasons. ▶ John married Sue **for (because of)** her money.
	When in doubt, use *because of*. *For* to express a reason is often ungrammatical. ▶ I didn't buy a ticket ~~**for**~~ **because of** the expense. ▶ I felt sick on the plane ~~**for**~~ **because of** turbulence.
	Only use *for* to express a reason when an *-ing* form follows. ▶ She was arrested **for** arguing with a police officer. ▶ I yelled at my brother **for not** turning off the lights.
To express a purpose	*For* is often used, however, to express purpose. ▶ I went to the store **for** some bread. ▶ I sent in the paperwork **for** my application.

3 Other ways of specifying do after 7.4

Either ... or, both ... and, and *not only ... but also*
You choose the music. **Either** Adele **or** Shakira is fine. I really like **both** Taylor Swift **and** Katy Perry. I listen **not only** to rock **but also** to jazz.

1A Make sentences with *so*, *such*, *so much*, or *so many*. Then suggest a solution for each problem.

1 ... noise outside that I can't sleep.
2 .... people with cars that it's impossible to park.
3 ... good desserts, but I can't eat any because I'm on a diet.
4 ... exciting to travel to new places, but I don't have any money.
5 .... homework that I'll never finish it all before Monday.
6 ... nice person, but when we didn't agree, he refused to speak to me.

There's so much noise outside that I can't sleep!

Why don't you just shut the window?

1B Make five sentences using one item in each column.

A	B	C
1 I walk to school	so as not to in order not to	burn out.
2 I call my parents every day		forget any vocabulary.
3 I take at least one vacation a year		have to wait for the bus.
4 I hardly ever go to museums		pay the entrance fee.
5 I read three books in English a year		worry them.

1C **Make it personal** Change three sentences in B so they are true. Share them. Any surprises?

I walk to school in order not to take the bus with my brother.

2A Correct the errors (1–6) in the story.

I was so excited that I was going to see Shakira in concert, but when we got to the stadium, the concert had been canceled (1) for rain. (2) Because of it had just started, the organizers were totally unprepared. No one wanted to go home, and one woman was arrested (3) because jumping over a fence. (4) For the chaos, I was really scared someone might get hurt. (5) Because of there had been no warning, everyone was so upset. I just went home and went right to sleep (6) for my disappointment.

2B Complete the sentences using *for* and the correct form of these reasons.

not come home on time	leave the refrigerator open	speak English	talk back to my boss	write the best essay

1 I was fired ____________. She said I was totally rude.
2 My mother yelled at me ____________. All of the food spoiled.
3 I got an award ____________. I really worked hard at it.
4 I felt proud of myself ____________. I was a little self-conscious of my accent, though.
5 I was punished ____________. My parents were so worried.

3A Make sentences using *either ... or*, *both ... and*, or *not only ... but also*.

1 English / Chinese
2 Brazilian music / Latino music
3 the guitar / the piano
4 modern art / impressionism
5 novels / mysteries

3B **Make it personal** Guess whether your partner's sentences are true. If you think they're false, correct them.

I speak both English and Chinese.

That's false. You speak both English and Spanish, though!

Bonus! Language in song

♫ Music makes the people come together. Music mix the bourgeoisie and the rebel.

- Correct a grammatical mistake in this song line.
- Combine the two sentences starting with since or because.

1 More on expressing ability do after 8.2

Present	I	**can / 'm able to**	speak five languages.	1
		can	give him a call now.	2
Past	I	**could / was able to**	see the ocean in the distance.	3
		was able to	get in touch with my brother.	4
Future	I	**'ll be able to**	speak French a year from now.	5
Present perfect	I	**can / 'll be able to**	see you tomorrow.	6
		've been able to	swim since I was three.	7
Verb + verb	I'd love to	**be able to**	come to your wedding.	8

Use *be able to*, but not *can*:
- for specific past events. (sentence 4)
- for something you will learn little by little. (sentence 5)
- with perfect tenses. (sentence 7)
- after another verb. (sentence 8)

Use *can*, but not *be able to*, when you offer to do something. (sentence 2)

2 Uses of *be supposed to* do after 8.2

We	**were supposed to**	arrive in the morning, but there was a delay.
I	**had to**	wait hours because I missed my connection.
We	**weren't supposed to**	have any of these headaches. I expected an easy trip!
I	**didn't have to**	be understanding, but I decided to be nice about it.

Be supposed to is often used to express something that turned out differently than expected. *Have to* is often used to express something that was inevitable.

Common mistake

The bus ~~had to~~ *was supposed to* be here at 2:30. Where is it?

3 Obligation and advice in the past do after 8.4

Obligation	I **had to** get a visa to enter Russia.	I **didn't have** to get a visa to go to Bermuda. My passport was good enough.
Strong advice	You'**d better** have packed some warm clothes before you left! It's freezing here.	I know you packed quickly, but you'**d better not have** forgotten your coat!
Advice	You **should have / ought to have** visited Times Square. Too bad you didn't.	You **shouldn't have** missed it. Well, too late now!

Remember! *Must have* in the past expresses probability, not obligation.
I **must have left** my passport at home. (= I'm pretty sure I left it at home.)

1A Circle the most logical options.

1 Don't worry. I [**can** / **'m able to**] speak to your brother today and ask for help.
2 I was terrified when the rollercoaster started its descent, but I [**could** / **was able to**] hold on tight.
3 Even though I can't cook very well now, I'm taking lessons, and I'm sure I [**can** / **'ll be able to**] cook next year.
4 Don't worry. I [**can** / **'m able to**] call the travel agency and ask if there's another flight.
5 I [**'ve been able to** / **can**] save money to buy a house, and I'm moving next week.
6 I'd like to [**can** / **be able to**] fly, but my heart starts to race at the thought of getting on a plane.

1B In pairs, which rules from 1 helped you choose the correct answer?

The first one sounds like an offer, so you have to use *can*.

2A Complete the sentences with the correct form of *have to* or *be supposed to* and the verbs.

1 Our plane ________ (arrive) by 10 p.m., but it didn't come in until midnight, so we ________ (spend) the night in a hotel.
2 I know Barry is difficult! He ________ (be) away today, but he came to work unexpectedly, so I ________ (invite) him to the picnic with everyone else.
3 My Mom ________ (be) here! If she hadn't come home early, she wouldn't have caught us looking at her computer.
4 My boyfriend ________ (meet) me at the airport, but he always thinks of others. He didn't want me to take the bus.
5 There was no parking at all! I ________ (drive) around the neighborhood for at least a half hour.
6 We ________ (get) our test results last Friday, but we didn't, so I ________ (live) with my anxiety all last weekend. I'm glad I passed in the end!

2B Make it personal Thinking on your feet! Share three things that you didn't expect to happen, but did. What did you do?

Well, I wasn't supposed to fail math because I did my homework every day, but when I did, I had to find a tutor.

3A Are these conversations logical? Correct the mistakes in the underlined words.

1 A: Oh, no! I can't find our passports. But maybe they're in this bag.
B: You <u>should have brought</u> them, or they won't let us on the plane. I reminded you three times!
2 A: I loved the U.S. It's a shame I didn't have time to go to the Grand Canyon.
B: You<u>'d better have found</u> time to go there. Who knows when you'll be back in Arizona.
3 A: Look at that rain! You <u>didn't have to leave</u> the windows open. Our carpet will be ruined!
B: Don't worry so much! I'm pretty sure I closed them.
4 A: I found out my license had expired, and I <u>should have taken</u> another driving test.
B: That sounds awful! I'm sure it's not what you were expecting.

3B Make it personal Share three fears and regrets using *(didn't) have to*, *had better (not) have*, and *was(n't) supposed to have*. Your partner will cheer you up.

I'd better not have left my car unlocked! It might be gone!

Bonus! Language in song

♫ How am I supposed to live without you? How am I supposed to carry on? When all that I've been livin' for is gone.

Grammatically, *can* and *be able to* can both replace *be supposed to* in this song line. Sing the line to yourself. Which one do you think sounds better?

1 Common prepositions ending relative clauses do after 9.2

I gave the plants **to** a neighbor.	→	That's the neighbor (who / that) I gave the plants **to**.
We used to live **in** this house.		It's near the house (that) we used to live **in**.
I arrived **at** this airport.		Your flight leaves from the airport (that) you arrived **at**.
John talked **about** the movie.		It was the movie (that) John talked **about**.
The thief was jailed **for** the robbery.		The thief regrets the robbery (that) he was jailed **for**.
He was convicted **of** a crime.		It's a crime (that) he was convicted **of**.
I went on a trip **with** Amy.		Amy is the friend (who / that) I went on a trip **with**.

Common mistake

He's the guy ~~with who~~ *(who)* I went to the party ^ *with*.

She's the woman I was talking ^ *to*.

In conversation, the preposition goes at the end. In very formal English, you may use *whom:* "I'm afraid it's a company **with whom** we no longer have relations."

2 Using relative clauses: summary do after 9.4

Restrictive
I finished the book (**that**) I was reading. My uncle is someone (**who / that**) I've always looked up **to**. Our school makes rules (**that / which**) I don't agree with.
Marcia is a good friend **who** comes over often. School is something **that** stresses me out.
Millenials are people **whose** values I really admire. I bought a car **whose** brakes don't work.
That's the house **where** I was born. It was a time **when** I was really happy.

Common mistake

He was late, ~~what~~ *which* upset me.
My dad, who is usually a sound sleeper, woke up when I came in.

You only have one dad. Remember to add the commas!

Restrictive, reduced
All those **standing** in the back, please exit through the rear door.
People **jogging** regularly may be prone to injuries.
Anyone **caught** entering will be arrested.

Non-restrictive
My grandfather, **who** is 70, bought his house in 1984.
People talk too loudly on their phones, **which** really annoys me.
We went to the theater last night, **where** we were surprised to see Martha.

More on relative pronouns

You can only delete a relative pronoun when the clause:

1 refers to the object of the sentence.
I finished the book. I was reading it. → I finished the book (that) I was reading.

2 refers to the subject of the sentence, *be* is also deleted, or the verb changes to an *-ing* form.
A person is speaking. The person is my son. → The person (who is) speaking is my son.

1A Circle the correct alternatives. Then complete the sentences.

1 Something I often worry [**about** / **for**] is ...
2 An issue I'm really interested [**about** / **in**] is ...
3 A time I got yelled [**at** / **to**] was when I ...
4 An event I'm really looking forward [**of** / **to**] is ...
5 Something really worth fighting [**to** / **for**] is ...
6 The hardest two things I've had to choose [**of** / **between**] are ...
7 The kind of person I'd like to get married [**to** / **with**] is ...
8 Something I've often wondered [**of** / **about**] is ...
9 A place I'd like to spend some time [**in** / **on**] is ...
10 A job I'm thinking of applying [**for** / **to**] is ...
11 Something I'm really hoping [**of** / **for**] next week is ...
12 Something I'm never really sure [**to** / **of**] is ...

1B **Make it personal** Share three sentences with a partner. Any surprises?

Something I often worry about is the future of our planet.

2A Add commas where necessary.

1 My only brother who's three years older than me wants to join the army.
2 Sally stepped on my foot three times which really made me mad!
3 We never think about the problems that we should worry about most.
4 My mother who's writing a novel always wanted to be a novelist.
5 Anyone who's caught cheating on this test will have to repeat the course. I mean it!
6 The man who I once almost married just got arrested.

2B Combine the two sentence with *who*, *that*, *which*, *whose*, *where* or *when*, and true information.

1 I'm fascinated by a country. The country is ...
A country which I'm fascinated by is Japan.
2 I most enjoy spending time with a friend. The friend is ...
3 I take vacations somewhere. The place is ...
4 I really like the sense of humor of someone in this class. The classmate is ...
5 I love a musician's albums. The musician is ...
6 People never ... It really annoys me.

2C ~~Cross out~~ all optional relative pronouns (and any other optional words). Then complete the sentences.

1 The best place that I've ever been to is ...
2 The politicians who are running this country ...
3 A writer whose books I love is ...
4 The type of weather that makes me depressed is ...
5 ... is an activity which I'd really like to be good at.
6 The person in my family who I confide in most is ...
7 These days many people think ... , which is exactly the opposite of what I think.
8 People who are caught stealing sometimes ...

2D In groups, share four opinions from B and C. Who do you have most in common with?

A country that really fascinates me is Japan.

Really? Tell me why. It's a place I know very little about.

Bonus! Language in song

♫ I'm all lost in the supermarket. I can no longer shop happily. I came in here for that special offer. A guaranteed personality.

Combine two of the sentences in this song line with *which*. Do you need a comma before *which*?

1 Responding to indirect questions, negative questions, and tag questions do after 10.2

Answers to all three types of questions may not include the words "yes" or "no," but the meaning is clearly implied.		
Indirect question	**Do you know if** you're coming over?	Sure. I said I would, remember? (= Yes.) Not yet. I'll call you later. (= I don't know.)
Negative question	**Aren't you going** to school today?	I'm leaving right now. (= Yes.) Actually, I'm not feeling well, so I think I'll stay home. (= No.)
Tag question	You have a doctor's appointment today, **don't you?**	It's tomorrow. (= No.) I'll give them a call now. (= I'm not sure.)

Other types of indirect questions may not even sound like questions. They are statements and end with a period, not a question mark.	
Excuse me, **I'm wondering** which way the train station is.	Just turn right at the corner.
I can't understand why checkout is at 11 a.m.	We have other guests arriving and need to clean the rooms.
I'm curious to know whether this bag is leather.	Yes, of course. It's 100% natural leather.
My hesitation is if there's a better discount elsewhere, to be honest.	I can guarantee that our prices are the lowest around.

2 Questions with *be used to*, *get used to*, and *used to* do after 10.4

Questions follow the same patterns as other question forms in the appropriate tenses.	
Present continuous	I wonder if they**'re** slowly **getting used to** the spicy food in Seoul.
Past of *be*	You **weren't used to** the cold weather, **were** you?
Simple past	**Didn't** you **use to live** around here?
Present perfect	You**'ve gotten used to speaking** English by now, **haven't** you?
Modal verbs	**Shouldn't** you **be used to** your husband's snoring by now? You've been married 25 years!
Future with *will*	**Will** I ever **get used to living** abroad?

1A Complete the questions with the words in parentheses in the correct order and form. Then write N (negative question), I (indirect question), or T (tag question).

1 *Why isn't there* a room available today? I had a reservation. (be – neg / there / why) *N*
2 I'm curious to know ________ the game last night. (win – past / we / whether)
3 Both you and Tom are going to the party tomorrow, ________? (be – neg / you)
4 ________ any smaller sizes? These are too big. (have – neg / you)
5 Do you have any idea ________ to London? I'm totally confused. (go / train / this / if)
6 ________ at this hotel before? He looks familiar. (stay – past, neg / that / guy)

1B Choose the most likely meaning for each response: *Yes*, *No*, or *I'm not sure*.

1 A: Isn't there a 20 percent discount on these pants?
B: Let me check with the manager.
2 A: Excuse me, could you tell me if there's a good restaurant on this street?
B: Actually, it's all residential down there.
3 A: We were in the same English class together last semester, weren't we?
B: You sure were a great student!
4 A: I can't understand why my car can't be fixed by tomorrow.
B: I'll take another look at our schedule.
5 A: I'd like to know whether these earrings are sterling silver.
B: For this price? But they're very attractive. I'm sure you'll enjoy them.
6 A: Hello, is this reception? I'm wondering if you can give me the WiFi password.
B: You're in Room 252? I'll call you in just a minute.

1C Choose three items and write three new sentences where B is a possible response.

2A Complete the sentences with a form of *be used to*, *get used to*, or *used to*.

1 A: I wonder if I ________ living here. It's so different from where I come from.
B: Give it time. I'm sure you will.
2 A: ________ work at Coffee Xpress, too? I'm positive I've seen you before.
B: No, but I was your next-door neighbor!
3 A: You ________ speaking English by now, haven't you? You've been in the U.S. for five years!
B: Not totally. I still wish I could speak French.
4 A: Your first winter in New York! ________ slowly ________ the cold weather and all the snow?
B: Little by little. But I'd still like to spend January on a beach in the Caribbean!
5 A: ________ travel more when you were younger?
B: No, I never traveled very much. I really didn't have the money.

2B Write three questions with *be used to*, *get used to*, or *used to* that you'd like to ask a classmate. Find the answers in your next class.

Bonus! Language in song

♫ Do you know where you're going to? Do you like the things that life is showing you? Where are you going to? Do you know?

Which song line is an indirect question? Which two lines can be rewritten as an indirect question?

1 More on reported speech do after 11.2

In some situations, the tense does not usually move back.
1 The statement is very recent. "I **want** to go to the movies tonight." → John said he **wants** to go to the movies tonight.
2 The statement is a universal truth. "The sun **rises** in the east and **sets** in the west." → My mother told me that the sun **rises** in the east and **sets** in the west.
3 The statement includes the modal verbs *might* and *should*. "I **might** go to Europe next summer." → Amy said she **might** go to Europe next summer. "We **should** call Mom more often." → They admitted they **should** call their mother more often.

Pronouns in reported sentences change to reflect the perspective of the speaker.

Direct sentence	Speaker	Reported sentence
"Why are **you** leaving?" Sarah's boss asked.	Sarah	My boss asked **me** why **I** was leaving.
	Sarah's friend	Sarah's boss asked **her** why **she** was leaving.

2 Reporting what people say do after 11.4

Notice the patterns possible for these verbs.

Verb	Correct	Incorrect	
I **said***	that I would call	~~her to call~~ ~~her that I would call~~	her parents.
I **told***	her that I would complain	~~to complain~~ ~~that I would complain~~	to her parents.
They **promised**	to keep that they would keep us that they would keep	~~us to keep~~	things secret.
They **agreed**	not to tell that they wouldn't tell	~~us not to tell~~ ~~wouldn't tell~~	anyone.
We **urged**	him to tell	~~to tell~~ ~~that he would tell~~ ~~him that he would tell~~	the truth.
He **threatened**	to call that he would call	~~her to call~~ ~~her that he would call~~	the police.
I **persuaded** We **begged**	them to tell	~~to tell~~ ~~that we would tell~~ ~~them that we would tell~~	their parents.

*Be careful! These sentences have different meanings. The second is a command.
"I'll call your parents." → I **said I would call** her parents.
"Call your parents." → I **said to call** her parents.

"I'll complain to your parents." → I **told her that I would complain** to her parents.
"Complain to your parents." → I **told her to complain** to her parents.

1A Change the sentences to reported speech. Pay careful attention to whether the tense moves back.

1 "You're going to get into trouble."
Sam warned Miles he ______________________.
2 "I'll be at the coffee shop in five minutes." (very recent statement)
Ellen said she ______________________.
3 "Stars only come out at night."
My teacher told us stars ______________________.
4 "I might be a little late tonight."
Phil reminded me he ______________________.
5 "I didn't tell anyone you and Ted broke up."
Melissa reassured me she ______________________.
6 "I didn't break the window!"
Eric denied he ______________________.

1B Report each sentence (a and b) using the correct pronouns.

1 "You can't take the day off, Sally."
a My boss told me ______________________.
b Sally told her parents ______________________.
2 "We're going to be moving, but we'll visit you often."
a My parents told me ______________________.
b My parents told their friends ______________________.
3 "What do you want?"
a The store owner asked us ______________________.
b The boys explained to the store owner ______________________.
4 "I don't have the rent money, so I can't pay you."
a My tenant Sue admitted to me ______________________.
b I told my landlady ______________________.

2A Correct the sentences so they are grammatical, paying attention to the underlined verbs. There may be more than one answer.

1 The guests noticed there had been a robbery, but they agreed me that they would stay calm.
The guests noticed there had been a robbery, but they agreed that they would stay (agreed to stay) calm.
2 Tim wasn't happy about lending me money, but I promised him to pay it back next week.
3 Lisa was very upset about failing her final exams, but I persuaded her that she wouldn't give up.
4 Bob had his credit cards stolen, but I urged him that he would keep his cool and call the bank to cancel them immediately.
5 Beth forgot all her lines during the play, and our director really lost it, but I begged him that he would give her a second chance.
6 Steve fell asleep in an important meeting, and his boss threatened him to fire him the next time it happened.
7 Our local TV station mispronounced my name, and I said them I wasn't happy at all about that.
8 Nancy's boyfriend is always asking her for money, and I told her stop seeing him.

2B Complete each sentence with the correct form of these verbs.

agree	beg	persuade	promise	threaten	urge

1 The way Larry __________ to call the police over a little loud music left me speechless. He shook his fist at us and started screaming!
2 Laura was caught looking through her boss's papers. I __________ her to apologize to him, but she just burst out laughing. (two answers)
3 George found a wallet on a bench. I urged him to try to find the owner, and eventually I __________ him to call the number inside.
4 Liz told me some juicy gossip, but I __________ not to tell a soul! So I really can't tell you, either. My lips are sealed. (two answers)

Bonus! Language in song

♫ You tell me that you're sorry. Didn't think I'd turn around and say that it's too late to apologize. It's too late.

Change the first sentence of this song line to reported speech beginning, "You told me that ... " and the second sentence (after "and") to reported speech beginning, "I said that ... "

Unit 12 Grammar expansion

1 More on predicting

do after 12.2

Both facts and predictions use *going to* or *will*.	
Fact	My sister **is going to be** / **will be** 21 in August.
Prediction	Checks **are going to** / **will disappear** within five years.

When you use the future continuous, you emphasize the ongoing nature of a prediction, but you may also use the future with *will*.	
Future with *will*	People **will live** on the moon by 2030.
Future continuous with *will*	People **will be living** there in small huts.

When you use the future perfect, you emphasize the completion of a prediction by a certain time. This tense is often used with *by the time*.	
Future perfect	By the time you get here, we **will have finished** dinner. Before the end of the year, I **will have spent** all my savings.

If you use *going to*, you sound more certain. Predictions based on present evidence often use *going to*.	
Future with *going to*	Global warming **is going to get** worse.
Future continuous with *going to*	We're **going to be paying** much higher rents a year from now. That's for sure!

When you are less sure of your prediction, you can use *may* or *might*.	
Future continuous with *might*	We **might all be living** on the moon a few years from now.
Future perfect with *may*	By 2050, they **may have sent** people to other planets, too!

Common mistake

Do not use the simple present or present continuous for predictions:

're going to spend / going to be spending
We ~~spend / 're spending~~ more by the end of the year.

2 More on the present continuous as future, *going to*, and *will*

do after 12.4

Use the present continuous as future or *going to* when your plan or decision is already made.
I'**m meeting** Pedro after class.
We'**re going to see** a movie.

However, if your plan is far in the future, use *going to:*
I'**m going to become** an engineer like my father.

Use the future with *will* when you're unsure about your plans:
I guess **we'll go** to the Rivoli for lunch.

Also use *will*, but not *going to* ...
1 when you make an offer or decide something as you're speaking:
- The phone's ringing. I'**ll get** it.

2 in stores and restaurants to express your intention:
- I'**ll take** the larger size.
- We'**ll** both **have** the fish.

3 to invite someone:
- **Will you join** us after class for coffee?

4 to make a promise:
- Officer, I promise **I won't speed** in the future!

1A Circle the best options.

1 A: Prices are through the roof! We [**'re going to be paying** / **'re paying**] even more by the end of the year.
B: That's for sure! We [**'ll be** / **'ll have been**] bankrupt soon.
2 A: Look how late we are! By the time we get to Bill and Marcy's, they [**will have left** / **will leave**] without us.
B: Stop worrying so much. I think they [**wait** / **'ll wait**] for us.
3 A: There [**are going to be** / **will be**] layoffs at our company. My boss told me!
B: Oh, no! We [**might be looking** / **might look**] for new jobs very soon!
4 A: By this time next year, we all [**will have graduated** / **will graduate**].
B: How can you be so sure? Maybe some of us [**will fail** / **will be failing**].

1B In pairs, answer these questions for each speaker in A. What other answers are possible?

- Is the event ongoing?
- Is it complete?
- Is the speaker sure?

In the first one, I think you can also say "We'll be paying ..." or even "We might be paying ... ." There's some evidence, but we can't be sure of the future.

2A Complete the conversations with a future form of the verbs in parentheses. There may be more than one answer.

1 A: ________ (you / come) to our party Saturday? We'd love to see you.
B: Oh, I wish I could, but I have some other plans.
2 A:I ________ (not do) it again! I promise.
B: That's what you said the last time! You ________ (not leave) home this weekend!
3 A: When I grow up, I ________ (study) architecture.
B: How can you be so sure? There are a lot of years between now and then.
4 A: What ________ (you / do) this weekend?
B: I ________ (go) camping. Helene invited me to go with her family.
5 A:Can I get you anything else?
B: No, I've decided. I ________ (take) the blue ones. Sorry to keep you waiting.
6 A: You failed your English exam? What happened?
B: I don't really know. I guess I ________ (talk) to my teacher on Monday and find out.

2B In pairs, try to explain the reasons for your choices in A before checking with your teacher.

In the first one, I chose will because it was an invitation: "Will you come to our party on Saturday?"

Oh, I decided the friend already knew about the party, so I chose "Are you coming to our party on Saturday?"

2C **Make it personal** Write three questions to ask a classmate about the future. How long can you continue the conversation?

What are you planning to do over the summer?

Bonus! Language in song

♫ I missed the last bus. I'll take the next train. I try but you see, it's hard to explain.

Rewrite the line "I'll take the next train" in two ways: (1) You've made a plan and have already bought your train ticket, and (2) You're not very sure what you'll do.

Selected audio scripts

7.7 *page 74 exercise 3C*

J = Josh, L = Liz

J: But the show was rescheduled, right?

L: It was, eventually, but I couldn't miss work again. But in September, she was scheduled to play in Mexico City and …

J: No! You …

L: You know, since I was on vacation, I thought I'd give her a second chance. Plus, I have friends there, so finding a place to stay wouldn't be a problem. Besides, …

J: Can't believe you went to Mexico! You lucky …

L: I did! So, anyway, I borrowed money for the tickets and …

J: I didn't know you were such a fan.

L: I am! Anyway, on the big day, I left home early so I'd have plenty of time to get to the airport.

J: Uh huh.

L: So I got on the plane and, guess what …

J: Engine failure!

L: No! But something was wrong with the air-conditioning and, well, we nearly froze to death, so the plane was diverted back to …

J: Kansas! No way!

L: Yep. I could have taken one the next day, but, you know, I was so fed up with the whole thing … I just gave up. It wasn't meant to be, I guess.

J: But …

L: In the end I downloaded the show just to have a taste of what I missed.

J: Sniff sniff. She'll go on another tour soon. Don't worry.

L: I hope so!

8.6 *page 84 exercises 3A and C*

D = Diego, L = Louise

D: So, in the end, did you go to Rita's party?

L: Yeah, Diego, but I wasn't able to get there until after 10, so I missed most of it.

D: How come?

L: Well, long story short there's a fence around our apartment complex, and, believe it or not, I couldn't get out.

D: What?

L: Yeah. I'd lost my key to the gate and couldn't find the spare one. So I couldn't get out onto the street!

D: That's so like you. But you were able to make it to the party …

L: Well, I climbed the fence and …

D: You what?

L: Yeah. My brother even took a photo. Look!

D: Why would he do that?

L: To embarrass me on Instagram®, obviously. You know him, Diego …

8.7 *page 84 exercises 3B and C*

D: But … I don't get it. Why didn't you simply call your parents?

L: I did! But there was no coverage where they were!

D: No way!

L: I know! I mean, what are the odds of that happening?

D: But, but … I thought you were afraid of heights.

L: Oh, no, on the contrary. Actually, in school, everyone used to call me spider girl, because, well … I could climb just about anything.

D: So you're telling me you were able to climb the fence? All dressed up like that?

L: Yeah.

D: Wow! I'm impressed. Did you at least enjoy the party?

L: Not exactly. I ran into Zack and his new girlfriend.

D: Oh, no! Of all people!

L: Yeah. I still have feelings for him, you know, and I think he could see it in my eyes … So that kind of spoiled the fun …

D: Hmm … it's been what since you broke up, a month or two?

L: Yeah. I still kind of miss him.

10.6 *page 106 exercise 3B*

Conversation 1

R = Receptionist, M = Marty

R: 6 a.m. to 10 a.m. Enjoy your stay, Mr. Falcon.

M: Thanks. Erm … one more thing, I was wondering if I could get a late checkout on Wednesday.

R: I'm sorry, but you need to check out by noon.

M: Listen, my flight doesn't leave until 5:00 … what am I supposed to do until then?

R: I'm really sorry, sir.

M: Can I speak to the manager, please?

R: Erm, she's on her lunch break.

M: Can you tell me what time she'll be back?

R: At around 2:00, sir.

M: Thank you.

R: My pleasure. Have a nice day!

M: Oh, by the way, I need a wake-up call tomorrow morning.

R: Of course. Just dial 000, set the time, and the system will wake you up.

M: You mean I have to use the phone in the room?

R: Yes, sir.

M: OK, thanks.

Conversation 2

S = Salesperson, M = Marty

S: … the green ones over there.

M: Would you happen to know whether these are machine-washable?

S: Yes, I think they are, sir.

M: You mean they won't shrink?

S: Let me take a look at the label just in case. Erm … it doesn't say anything. I'll check with the manager.

M: No need to, thanks. They're \$19.99, aren't they, you said?

S: Erm … No, \$90.99 plus tax.

M: How much?

S: \$90.99.

M: Wow! Over a hundred dollars?! That's a rip-off! Aren't these things supposed to cost about 20 bucks?

S: Actually, \$90.99 is less than the suggested retail price, sir. They're 100 percent cotton.

M: Really? Wow! If you say so … Well, OK, I'll take them.

S: Great! How would you like to pay?

M: Do you accept international credit cards? I'm living in London now.

S: Sure. Sir, I'm afraid your card didn't go through.

M: Really? That's weird. I use this card all the time.

S: Yeah.

M: Erm … Can you try again, please?

S: Oh, of course. No, sorry. Don't you have another card?

M: Yeah. Do you …

Conversation 3

F = Fiona, M = Marty

F: Spencer and White Rent a Car. Fiona speaking. How may I help you?

M: Erm … My car broke down and I don't know what to do. I'm lost in the middle of nowhere.

F: OK. The fastest way to report a car breakdown is via our app. Do you know whether you have it installed on your phone? That way, we'll know exactly where you are and send someone over.

M: Yeah, but I don't have a login or a password. Can't you help me over the phone?

F: Erm, just a minute. Please hold. … Yes, sir, I can now help you! Could I have your name, please?

M: Marty Falcon.

F: And your reservation number?

M: 8983F.

F: It says "invalid reservation number."

M: What do you mean? It's the number on the document.

F: Hmm … It seems there's been a mix up. Hmm … Let me see if I can correct it and fix things up. Hold the line, please. …Thanks for holding. Mr. Falcon, do you remember if any warning lights came on?

M: Warning lights? You mean something that lights up red or is it blue? – like on the dashboard?

F: Yes.

M: Well, yeah, the "check engine" light was on, but, er, I figured it was nothing serious, so I just …

F: I see. Do you know what your exact location is?

M: No, I don't! I'm *completely* lost and in the middle of nowhere.

F: OK. Hold the line, please.

10.12 *page 111 exercise 9C*

Mariana from Caracas, Venezuela

I love Vermont … and the campus … But, well, I was born and raised in Caracas, so I kind of miss the hustle and bustle of life there – you know, the noise, the crowds, even the traffic! I'm sure I'll get used to the peace and quiet eventually... Well, at least I hope so. The upside, though, is that life here is generally healthier ... plus, I'm no longer the couch potato I used to be, which is a good thing, of course.

Ignacio from Montevideo, Uruguay

I grew up in a big house, so my sisters and I had our own bedrooms ... So, erm, I'm not used to sharing a room with anyone – let alone someone I barely know. Besides, my roommate isn't very talkative, which doesn't exactly help. He's so quiet it's weird sometimes. I mean, it's been two months and we, erm, we hardly know each other. Not that I've tried too hard, to be honest, so I guess it's my fault as much as his. Mom says we'll get used to living together. I hope she's right.

Ines from Lisbon, Portugal

It's, erm, it's been tough. I'm fresh out of high school, where there was, you know, far more hand-holding and guidance. So, erm, I guess in many ways I'm not used to being treated as an adult. Also, at school our final grade was based mostly on exams. Here we have regular assignments, quizzes, projects and exams, which can be a little overwhelming. I wonder if I'll ever get used to working this hard. Plus, you need a lot of self-discipline, which is definitely not my strong suit.

Diego from Bogota, Colombia

My father got transferred to Miami when I was little boy, and we lived there for, what, three years, so, erm, well, when I came here, I was used to life in the States ... I mean, there was less of a culture clash than I'd anticipated. But ... it took me a while to get used to the weather. It's freezing in Vermont in the winter! You have no idea, and it snows constantly. I was used to a mild climate. I even had to buy a whole new wardrobe!

Elena from Moscow, Russia

The first few weeks were kind of fun, but then I started to feel terribly homesick. I wasn't used to being away from my parents for more than couple of days. I'm an only child, and we're a very close-knit family and, well, even though we Skype at least once a week and What'sApp constantly, it's not really the same. They try to act strong, but deep down I know they wish they could catch the first plane and take me back home.

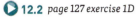

12.2 *page 127 exercise 1D*

A = Announcer, R= Rob, L = Lisa, M = Mike, T = Teresa

A: We're ready to survey our first guest over here on the right. And your name is ...

R: Rob.

A: OK, Rob, let's begin by talking about school tests. You said you're 19, so that means you're in college?

R: Uh huh, it's my second year.

A: How optimistic are you about your exams?

R: You mean my finals?

A: Yeah.

R: Hmm ... I haven't been putting a lot of effort into my work and it, it turns out I've had a couple of Fs ... I keep telling myself that it's not the end of the world if I fail an exam or two, but deep down, I know I'll be really upset.

A: So what are you going to do about it?

R: I guess I'd better start studying. Anyway, I'm keeping my fingers crossed.

A: So you're "unsure" about your exams?

R: You could say that again!

A: Let's try someone else. OK, in front. Your name?

L: Lisa.

A: Good. Let me ask you Lisa ... how optimistic are you about your career?

L: Well, I'm studying pharmacy, and right now I have a part-time job at ID drugs.

A: The drugstore chain?

L: Uh huh. It's great training. But they're going through a rough time right now, so who knows what the future has in store for me. If they have to let some people go, I'm pretty sure I'm at the top of the list. I mean, I've been there for less than a year, and I haven't even graduated from college yet.

A: Hmm ... So it doesn't look good?

L: Nope.

A: I'm sorry to hear that! What about your future in general?

L: All I can tell you is I'm feeling pretty down right now.

A: Let's try someone else. And you're ...

M: Mike.

A: OK, Mike. How optimistic are you about your team's chances of winning the championship?

M: You mean soccer?

A: Well, it could be any sport, soccer, football, baseb...

M: Hmm ... well, my soccer team hasn't been doing too well. We haven't won a single game.

A: You haven't?

M: No, but ... well, I know we've lost all the games so far this season, but now with this new coach, there might be a light at the end of the tunnel. I'm trying not to let it get me down.

A: Does that mean you're optimistic?

M: I just have no idea really, to be honest.

V Time for just one more. You, over here. And your name?

T: Teresa.

A: OK, Teresa, how optimistic are you about the country's economy?

T: Well, it sort of depends on who you ask, doesn't it? If you watch the eight o'clock news, you get the impression that we're on the brink of chaos. I mean, the ... the media tends to blow things out of proportion but, on the whole, I think we're doing OK. Anyway, I try to keep my feet on the ground and save a little every month, you know, just in case. But I think we're definitely headed in the right direction.

A: Thank you. You're a lot more confident than I am!

iDentities

Richmond

WORKBOOK

How important is music to you?

A Complete the biography with these words. There are two extra words.

came	high-profile	large	lost	regarded	released	rose	took

Taylor Swift is ¹__________ as one of the finest singer-songwriters of the decade. Born in Reading, Pennsylvania on December 13th, 1989, she moved to Nashville, Tennessee at the age of 14 to pursue a career in country music. She ²__________ to fame through the hit *Our Song*, which she wrote when she was still a teenager. She became the youngest songwriter ever signed by Sony® and ³__________ her debut album, *Taylor Swift*, when she was only 16. By the time her second album *Fearless* ⁴__________ out in 2007, she was already one of the biggest stars on the U.S. rock and pop scene. It was named album of the year at the Grammys, making her the youngest-ever winner of the award.

As a ⁵__________ figure in the music industry, Swift is also prepared to speak out on important issues, such as the payment of royalties by Apple® for online downloads. This dispute ⁶__________ place in 2015 when a single online letter from Swift changed Apple's policy in just one day. As someone who was fighting for the rights of less successful artists, Swift gained even more fans for her brave act in standing up to big business. Her fifth album, *1989*, was the world's second-biggest seller in 2015, beaten only by Adele's *25*.

B 26 Circle the correct alternatives. Listen to check.

LISA: I've ¹*done / had* enough of this album. You play it all the time.

SHANE: I know, I'm sorry. For some reason, I just can't ²*get / make* enough of it.

LISA: What is it about you and Taylor Swift?

SHANE: Her music is amazing. I also like her because she's been on a similar musical path to me.

LISA: Yeah, right. You're hardly a multi-million-download-selling hit machine!

SHANE: I'm talking about musical styles. Taylor Swift started her career as a country and western singer. Then she changed to pop. Well, when I was a kid, I was really fond ³*about / of* country music. My mom and dad were in a band, and we listened to country all the time. They were the New Jersey Cowboys.

LISA: You're kidding!

SHANE: Not at all! They were really good. Anyway, eventually I ⁴*got / took* tired of listening to all those songs, and I started listening to other things. Now, I'm hooked ⁵*in / on* rock, and I think Taylor Swift is one of the best performers out there.

LISA: I don't know. I'm more ⁶*into / onto* funky stuff like Bruno Mars. In fact, I'm switching tracks now. It's time for a bit of *Uptown Funk*!

SHANE: Fine, but I'll change it back as soon as you go out!

C Make it personal Complete these sentences about musical tastes so they're true for you.

When I was a kid, I was fond __________________, but now I'm hooked __________________.

I never get tired of __________________. I can't get enough __________________.

What was your most recent disappointment?

A Match 1–6 to a–h to make a story. There are two extra endings.

1 We were determined to see Adele in concert since
2 The concert was on the same day as my eldest daughter's birthday, so
3 On the day, we were late for the concert because of
4 Then my youngest daughter couldn't see much because
5 I put her on my shoulders so that
6 We loved it, but we can't go to her next concert due to

a ☐ all the cars on the road.
b ☐ the high price of the tickets.
c ☐ I decided to get some tickets as a present.
d ☐ there were so many tall people in front of her.
e ☐ the tickets were too expensive.
f ☐ she was able to see the stage.
g ☐ there were so many cars on the road.
h ☐ she hadn't toured in years.

B Read and cross out the incorrect choice for 1–6.

What was your most recent disappointment?

Last month and it was massive! All my life I had wanted to see the musical *Cats*, but it had been impossible 1*as / since / so that* the producers had stopped the shows back in the year 2000. 2*Because / Because of / As* I heard they were bringing it back to the stage this year, I was determined to see it.

We bought the tickets, and we were all ready to go to Broadway to see it on Thanksgiving. That morning, my dad was putting some pictures up 3*due to / in order to / to* make the house look nice before our grandma visited the next day. Unfortunately, he put a nail right through a water pipe. Water was pouring into the living room. It was a disaster, and we couldn't find a plumber 4*because of / due to / since* the holiday. We waited for ages and ended up missing the show. My dad promised to get new tickets 5*in order to / so / so that* we could go another day, but *Cats* was only on for a limited time. 6*As / Because of / Due to* that, I never got to see the show. What a bitter disappointment!

C Correct the mistake in each sentence. One sentence is correct.

1 I didn't buy a ticket for the concert, so I didn't hear about it in time. ______
2 We set off early in order beat the morning rush-hour traffic. ______
3 They postponed the final game due to the weather. ______
4 I'm going to the supermarket for get some fruit. ______
5 So that he was so unfit, his doctor advised him to go to the gym twice a week. ______

A Read the article. T (true) or F (false)?

1 Movies that critics really don't like are certain to be unpopular with the general public.
2 Some movies might fail in the U.S. but, nevertheless, be very successful in the rest of the world.

B Re-read and complete 1–5 with the missing sentences a–e.

a 2013's *After Earth* is another classic example.
b Anything that originally came from a comic seems like box-office gold.
c Not such a bad piece of business after all.
d they are unbelievably expensive to make
e While they often disagree,

Think they're flops? Actually they're not!

1________, there are some movies that the critics unanimously hate. As soon as they hit the big screen, the attack begins. It doesn't take long for a movie to get a reputation as a complete **dud** – but actually many movies that people think are flops have made a huge amount of money.

One of the most famous disasters of all time was 1995's *Waterworld*. This movie takes place in the future after the Antarctic has **melted** and the world is almost completely underwater. It was hugely expensive to make, and people said it lost a fortune. However, a flop it was not – *Waterworld* eventually made a **profit** of $91 million. 2________

Nowadays, superhero movies are a license to print money. 3________ Back in 2006, they weren't such a **guaranteed** hit. That year's *Superman Returns* was widely considered to be a failure, but it too made around $130 million. If that's a failure, give some to me!

The key thing here is that these are worldwide hits. Some of these movies failed at home in the U.S., but drew enormous audiences **overseas**. 4________ This adventure on a distant planet starred real-life father and son Will and Jaden Smith. While U.S. audiences stayed at home, the movie made $182 million in the rest of the world. Strangely, even Will Smith considers the film to be a disaster, despite its global success.

It's no coincidence that these are all science-fiction movies. Because of their special effects, 5________. If they don't make instant millions, it's easy to say that they are failures, especially during their opening weekend. Nevertheless, it's increasingly obvious that the media isn't always right: when they label a movie a flop, a lot of times, it's not.

C Match the bold words in the article to definitions 1–5.

1 money you earn from something ________
2 a movie that is a flop, not a success ________
3 definite, certain ________
4 changed from a solid to a liquid ________
5 in other countries ________

D 27 Complete 1–5 with these words. There's one extra. Listen to check.

backfired	caught on	didn't live up to	failed to	lacked	surprised

1 The restaurant hoped that people would love their super-spicy pizza with extra chili, but it never ________. Nobody seemed to like it.
2 The musical was OK, but it ________ really powerful songs. What it really needed were some catchy ones for audiences to sing along with.
3 We thought that the concert was going to be amazing, but sadly it ________ our expectations. Really disappointing.
4 Stacey posted a photo on Facebook of me singing to make fun of me – but her plan ________. Everybody loved it. I got over 100 likes!
5 The band's first album ________ impress people, but their second album was a huge hit!

When was the last time you went to a museum?

A 28 Listen to a podcast between James and Adriana about an exhibit at the Tate Modern art gallery in London. Number the verbs in the order you hear them (1–4).

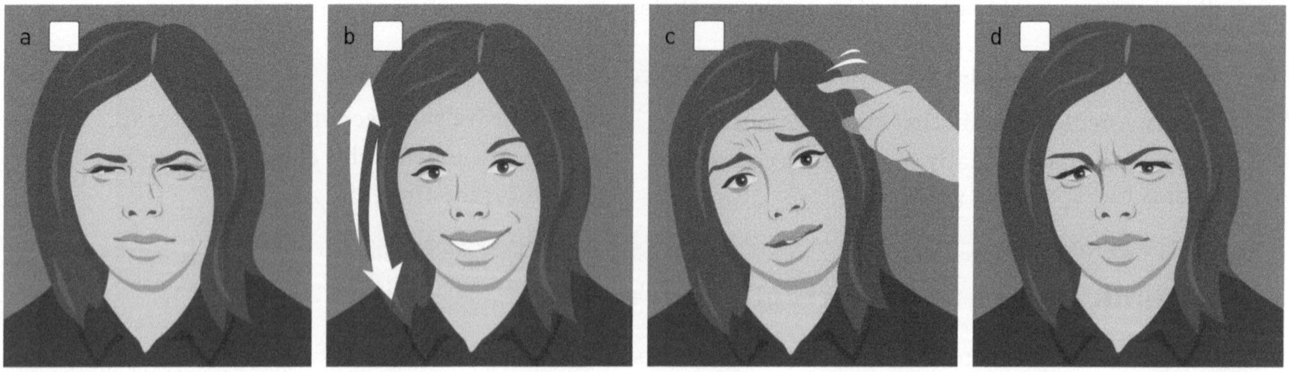

B 28 Listen again. T (true) or F (false)?

1 Adriana is a fan of Modern Art.
2 The Tate Modern building has always been an art gallery.
3 The slide was invented by a British artist.
4 In the beginning, the kids didn't have enough tickets for the slide.
5 You have to wear protective clothing on the slide.
6 James wanted to go on the slide several times.
7 The slide is art because it makes people feel strong emotions.
8 The slide has only appeared in museums in Europe.

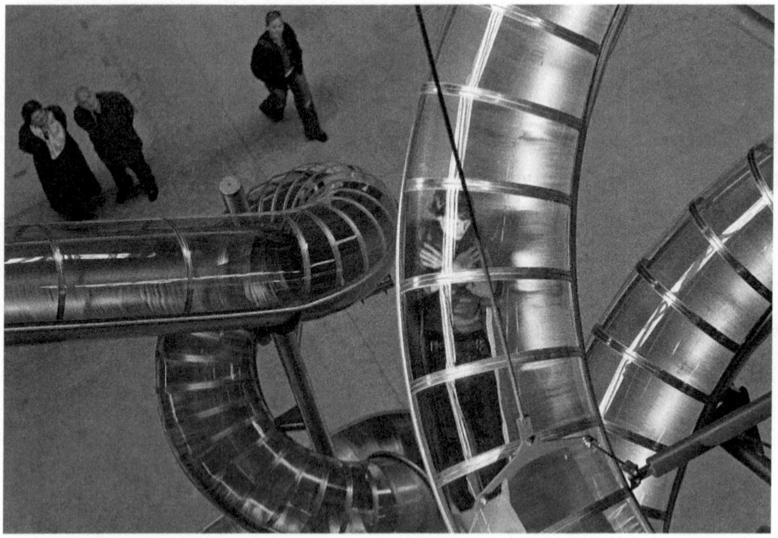

C Correct the mistake in each sentence. One sentence is correct.

1 We have another students in our class today. ______
2 Some other people was in the gallery at the same time as us. ______
3 Do you like this painting or the others ones? ______
4 I can't meet at 4 p.m. Can you meet at other time? ______
5 I like the hotels in the city center, but I don't like the other. They're too far away. ______
6 My son made friends with some other children when we were on holiday. ______
7 Can you help me, please? There's another problem with the computer. ______
8 Harry is going to study medicine – and I have some others news for you, too. ______

Writing a review

A Complete the review with the adverb form of these words.

absolute	clever	consistent	disappoint	easy	firm	huge	~~incredible~~	occasion	surprise

George Ezra – Live in Spain!

A George Ezra's biggest hit *Budapest* has already gotten 113 million listens on Spotify®, and [1] *incredibly* he's still only 23.

B Barcelona [2]________ gets big acts playing in the city, such as Coldplay and U2. They play in enormous venues like the Nou Camp, FC Barcelona's stadium. However, Ezra was in the Sala Bikini, a [3]________ small place for someone with his online success. We were just five meters from the stage in a room that was as big as a restaurant. It was [4]________ the closest I've ever been to such a big star in concert.

C We arrived late, so [5]________ we missed the support act, but Ezra came on stage right on time. The opening song was *Cassy O*, the fastest track from his [6]________ successful album *Wanted on Voyage*. The crowd was rocking from the start.

D His voice was [7]________ amazing throughout the whole concert. We loved the gig. The two highlights of the night were *Budapest*, of course, as well as *Barcelona*. Ezra wrote the song about a visit to our city, and [8]________ he left it till the very end.

E Live, Ezra is [9]________ incredible, and I [10]________ believe that in the future he's going to be a mega-star. Get to see him in small venues while you still can!

B In which paragraph A–E do you find the answers to 1–6? One question is not answered.

1 What albums has George Ezra recorded? ☐
2 What were the best parts of the concert? ☐
3 What nationality is George Ezra? ☐
4 Where can you see live music in Barcelona? ☐
5 Does the author recommend seeing George Ezra in concert? ☐
6 How old was George Ezra when he played in Barcelona? ☐

C **Make it personal** Write a one-paragraph review of a concert you saw. Include this information: Who? Where? When? Best parts?

____

____

____

D Look back at lessons 7.1–7.5 in the Student's Book. Find the connection between the song lines and the content of each lesson.

E ▶29 Listen to the five question titles from the unit, and record your answers to them. If possible, compare recordings with a classmate.

Has fear ever held you back?

A Combine ideas 1–6 into single sentences using the words in CAPITALS.

1 I have a fear of flying. I cannot get on a plane. TERRIFIED
I'm terrified of flying.

2 I think prawns are disgusting. They look like insects to me. FREAK / OUT
____

3 I don't have a problem with snakes. Unlike many people. BOTHER / ME
____

4 You can bring your dog when you stay with us. I really like them. MIND / AT ALL
____

5 I try not to give presentations on my job. I get too nervous. AVOID
____

6 I always feel uncomfortable around spiders. I don't know why. MAKE / BIT / UNEASY
____

B 30 Complete the blog with these words. There are two extra. Listen to check.

breathe	dizzy	fell	heart	neck	passed	stomach	sweat	tears

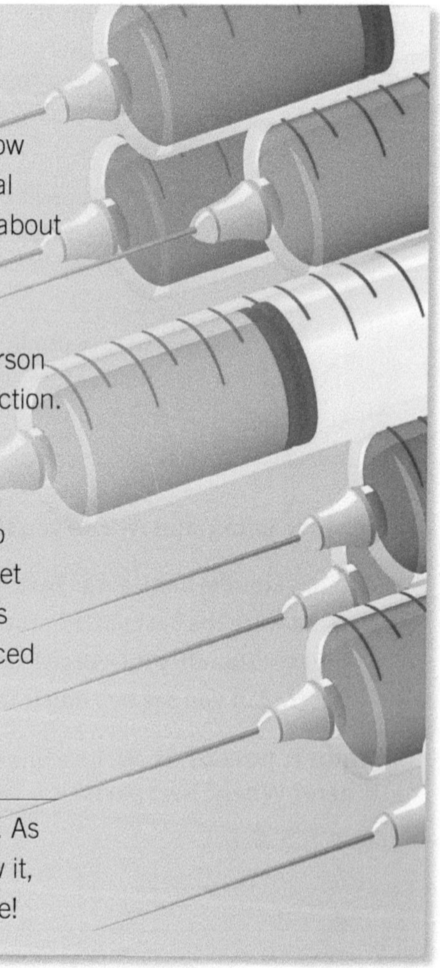

Jabs needle me!

What a day! I'm off to South America next month and had to get a yellow fever vaccination. I'd been panicking about it for weeks as I have a total phobia of needles. My [1] ______________ starts to race just thinking about injections because of a really nasty experience at school.

When I was about 14, we all had to have a BCG injection against tuberculosis, and the nurse was horrible. She made us watch each person in turn get the injection. I waited, terrified, staring at injection after injection. I almost [2] ______________ out in terror. In the end, I burst into [3] ______________ , and all the other kids laughed at me.

So today was awful. My girlfriend, Susie, came with me, but I started to [4] ______________ even before we got to the doctor's. My shirt was wet as if it was 35°C outside. While we were waiting, I got terrible butterflies in my [5] ______________ . I wanted to run out the door, but Susie forced me to stay.

Finally, the doctor called me in. When I saw the needle, I got really [6] ______________ . My head was spinning. I couldn't [7] ______________ – I wanted my asthma inhaler, but then something amazing happened. As the doctor was chatting with me, she walked behind me. Before I knew it, the injection was over, in a flash! So, Amazon rainforest – here we come!

C Make it personal Complete the sentences so they're true for you.

1 When I see a needle, I ______________________________ .

2 Once I burst into tears because ______________________________ .

3 I often get butterflies in my stomach before ______________________________ .

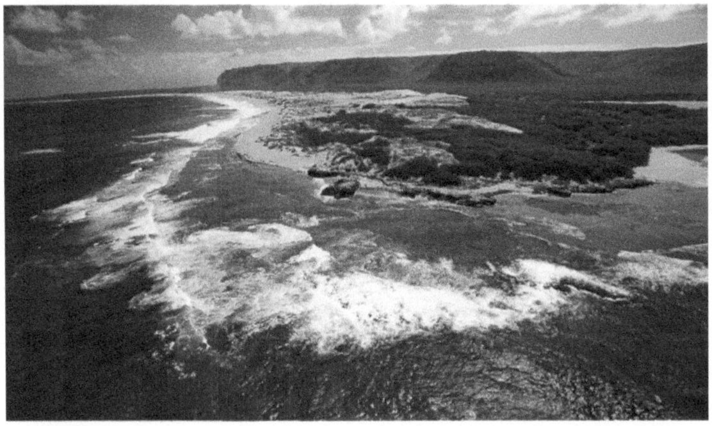

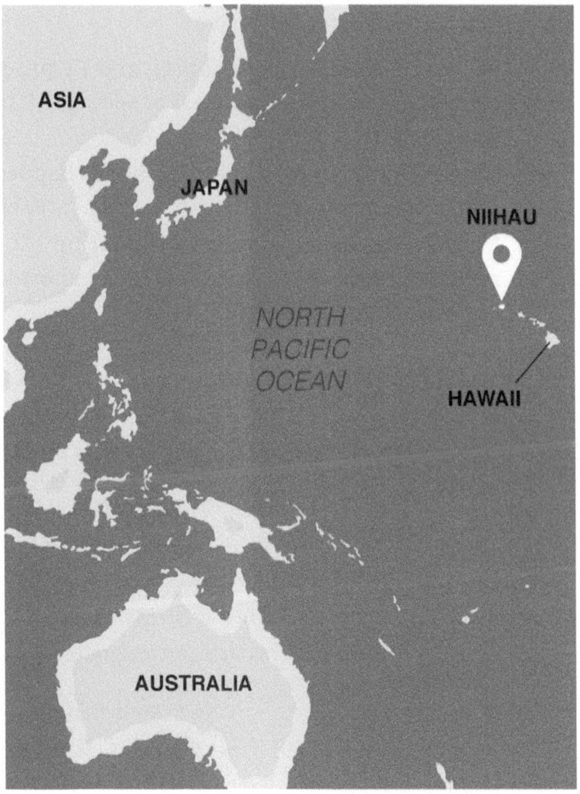

A 31 Listen to a conversation about Niihau, Hawaii's "forbidden island." Who said 1–6: M (Martina) or L (Luca)?

1 For many years, tourists couldn't go to Niihau at all. ☐
2 Are you telling me you were able to visit this place? ☐
3 Were you able to meet any of the locals? ☐
4 Our limit was three hours. ☐
5 I was just able to take a photo before it disappeared under the water. ☐
6 I don't think I could have done it on my own. ☐

B 31 Correct one word in each sentence. Listen again to check.

1 That's because it's one of the most unpleasant places in the world to visit. ________
2 In the past, you could only go there if you worked there. ________
3 I managed to go there by boat with my parents. ________
4 No one speaks English on the island. ________
5 The sea is crystal clear, and the beaches have wonderful golden sand. ________
6 There are only a few trips to Niihau every month. ________
7 My company paid for me to go there. It was very expensive. ________
8 It was the most terrifying experience of my life. ________

C Complete conversations 1–5 with *could* or *was able to*. Use both when possible.

1 A: Did you see that Nicky was on TV last night?
B: Yeah! I ________ believe it!
2 A: Are you having a nice stay in L.A.?
B: Yes, the hotel has a cool pool, so I ________ have a great swim yesterday.
3 A: Mom, what was my first word?
B: Well, you ________ speak at about 18 months old, and as far as I remember, it was "daddy."
4 A: Did you get Jimi's birthday present?
B: Yes, just! I got to the store as it was closing, so I ________ quickly buy him a book.
5 A: Where have you been? Did you get lost?
B: Yeah, we ________ get the sat-nav to work in the car. I think it's broken.

D **Make it personal** Write true answers to these questions.

1 Was there anything you could do as a child that you can't do now?

____

2 Was there anything you weren't able to do last year that you really wanted to do?

____

How much attention do you pay to the news?

A Circle the correct alternatives.

1 News editors, photojournalists, and TV producers have to *carry out / cope with* the stress of seeing disturbing images as part of their jobs.

2 Nevertheless, when something bad is happening, the media has a responsibility to *spread / carry out* the news.

3 More and more violence is appearing on TV, and studies need to be *boosted / carried out* to learn how these changes are affecting our society.

4 The use of extreme scenes is a cynical way of *boosting / coping with* a show's ratings.

5 That is how rumors are *boosted / spread*.

6 Many viewers of the news may be *spreading / undergoing* treatment with medical professionals for stress-related illnesses.

B Read and complete the webpage, with topic sentences 1–6 from **A**. There's one extra.

How real should the news be?

A________ It's especially a problem in drama where almost every series contains graphic images with little warning for the viewer. Whatever the conclusions of future research, it seems clear that things that were shocking for our grandparents have become an everyday occurrence in modern drama.

B________ It gets everybody talking about the series, both with their friends and on social media. Newspapers run stories about it pretending to criticize the action while printing photos of the most explicit scenes. The public seems to have an insatiable appetite for this kind of violence. But what about real violence and real suffering?

C________ Indeed, they come across much worse scenes every day than they ultimately show to the public. They then edit these for broadcast. Now the question is, how graphic should the news be? Should they show the true horror of violence that professionals in the field encounter? Clearly, the answer has to be "no".

D________ Unlike in a drama where people know what kind of images they are likely to see, any viewer can just switch on the news. Seeing graphic images of violence without warning can badly affect people who have lived through terrible events in their own lives. Shocking images can bring back their own experiences.

E________ Otherwise, the public can close its eyes and pretend that the troubles of the world aren't really happening. This leads to a difficult balancing act for TV producers and newspaper editors. On the one hand, they are presenting news for an "unshockable" public that is used to seeing graphic images. On the other, they have a responsibility towards younger and more impressionable viewers. This tension is what prevents the news from being as "real" as it could be.

C Use the clues to complete the puzzle. What is the adjective in gray?

1 Failed TV stars will go on any old reality show to boost their ______ with the public.

2 Singing in front of an audience for the first time has boosted my ______ enormously. I now really believe in myself.

3 I told my granddad that I would get into medical school, and I'm determined to carry out the ______ that I made to him.

4 Our company is undergoing a lot of ______ at the moment. Things are different from one day to the next.

5 Janine has been spreading ______ about me. She told everyone that I'd been stealing from the company, and it's just not true.

6 I'm finding it difficult to cope with the ______ of bringing up two small children. Being a mother is the hardest job in the world.

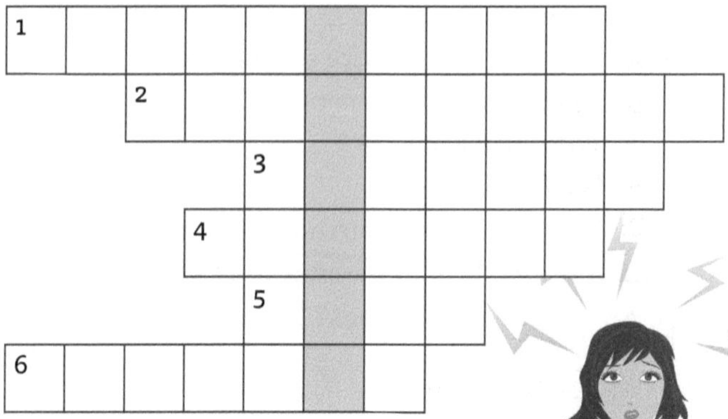

A Match 1–4 to a–e to complete the sentences. There's one extra ending.

1 You aren't allowed to drive when you're taking this medication. It's a
2 You can use cell phones, but you can't use laptops on planes. That just seems contradictory. It's a
3 Technically, it's forbidden to use your cell phone at customs, but they don't
4 In most countries, you have to carry an ID card at all times. It's

a ☐ enforce the law.
b ☐ got to obey.
c ☐ pointless law.
d ☐ violation of the law.
e ☐ required by law.

B Check (✓) the signs that match the rules. Correct those that don't.

1

2

3

4

5

6

1 You're supposed to eat here. ☐ ______________
2 No dogs are allowed on the beach. ☐ ______________
3 You'd better watch out for penguins while you're driving. ☐ ______________
4 You don't have to swim here. ☐ ______________
5 You should drink the tap water. ☐ ______________
6 Only disabled people aren't allowed to park here. ☐ ______________

C ▶32 Complete the conversations with these words. There's one extra. Listen to check.

're allowed to	aren't supposed to	must not	'd better	don't have to	ought to

1 A: I ate that last sandwich in the fridge, and now I've found out that it was Ella's!
B: Well, you ______________ not tell her it was you. She'll be furious.
2 A: Do I need to wear a tie for the meeting?
B: No, you ______________. Everyone just wears casual clothes, but it's up to you.
3 A: I need to find my hotel reservation. Can I look up the address on your computer?
B: Well, we ______________ do that at work, but I guess it's OK, just this once. But don't tell anyone or I'll get in trouble!
4 A: Do you have any recommendations for things to do while I'm in Athens?
B: You ______________ go to the archaeological museum. It's amazing! And it's only about seven euros to get in!
5 A: Is it OK to use my cell phone here in the hospital?
B: You ______________ use them outside, in the corridors and café, but not on the wards themselves. Besides, it's often hard to get a signal.

D **Make it personal** Complete 1–5 to make true statements about your workplace / place of study.

1 We are / aren't supposed to ______________, but nobody does it.
2 Everyone is allowed to ______________.
3 We have to ______________ every day.
4 At lunchtime, we can ______________.
5 You shouldn't ______________ at any time.

A message of advice

A Read Ivana's response to George. Check (✓) the things that George mentioned in his previous message to Ingrid.

George ...

1 asked her to give him some advice. ☐
2 told Ingrid he was feeling stressed. ☐
3 has a new job. ☐
4 has lots of friends where he lives. ☐
5 feels unwell because of his anxiety. ☐
6 loves doing all kinds of sports. ☐
7 feels tired all the time. ☐
8 doesn't use Skype®. ☐

So, if you have any advice, Ingrid, I'd love to hear it. Hope to hear from you soon.

George

Hi George

Lots of us suffer from anxiety. I [1]m__ __n it's normal to feel like this when you start out on a new career, like you are. Fortunately, there are lots of ways to combat this problem.

[2]F__ __ st__ __t__ __s, you're doing the right thing to ask for advice. Many people feel alone because they bottle these feelings up, [3]s__ t__ sp__ __k. Just talking about your fears can help you cope with them. It's a shame you have nobody close to you in your new home.

A common experience is physical symptoms of anxiety such as sweating and feeling dizzy. [4]Th__ __ sa__ __, many of us have difficulty breathing when we feel stressed, and you need to learn to control that. Breathing exercises can really help to calm you down. [5]T__ __ __t me, these will help to control those feelings of panic.

Another technique is to do some exercise. You said you enjoy running, so maybe you should go for a run now and then. When you live in the moment, you forget your worries for a while. [6]O__ __ __r th__ __ th__ __, when I feel anxious, I always take the dog for a walk, and that really helps.

In fact, living a healthy lifestyle is very important in terms of our mental health. Make simple changes. You said you weren't sleeping well even though you were often exhausted. You shouldn't drink coffee or tea or too many sodas. They contain caffeine, and they can stop you sleeping at night. [7]N__ __dl__ __ __ to s__ __, when you're anxious, you have to get plenty of rest.

If you want to talk about anything else, you can call me anytime, OK? [8]Th__ __ __ g__ __d__ __ __s we have Skype!

Ingrid

B Complete the missing letters in the phrases for making friendly comments.

C Underline the five pieces of advice Ingrid gives George. Then think of your own advice for George.

A couple of other things you could try doing are ________________________________
and ____.

D Look back at lessons 8.1–8.5 in the Student's Book. Find the connection between the song lines and the content of each lesson.

E ▶33 Listen to the five question titles from the unit, and record your answers to them. If possible, compare recordings with a classmate.

How much time do you spend on your own?

A Read and complete the article with these words and phrases. There are two extra words/phrases.

keep quiet	mingle	open up	reveal	small talk	thinking it over	thinking out loud

How to survive at a wedding when you don't have anyone to go with

- First of all, you should [1] ________________ when you arrive and chat with everyone you can. You'll be surprised how many other people also feel like strangers at an event like this.
- It's a mistake to [2] ________________ when you're on your own. You have to initiate conversations and start talking.
- If you find it difficult to make [3] ________________, just ask lots of questions: *What do you do? How did you decide what to wear?*
- If you're embarrassed about being alone, just don't tell anyone. You don't have to [4] ________________ any information about yourself. Anyway, what's wrong with being alone? Everyone's single at some point in his or her life.
- The hardest part is the dancing. My advice is to prepare for this early on. At the buffet or during the welcome drinks, do some [5] ________________ about what you're going to do when all the couples are on the dance floor. Someone will hear you and is sure to be in the same situation. You'll soon find a non-dancing buddy to chat with while everyone else is having his or her romantic moment.

B 34 Order the words in B's responses to questions about plans for a wedding. Listen to check.

1 A: What do you think of Vicky's suggestion of San Francisco for your honeymoon?
B: the / over / it / of / thinking / we're / process / in
____
____

2 A: How does Mike know about the bachelor party? It's supposed to be a secret.
B: mistake / showed / invitation / him / by / I / the / to
____
____

3 A: Did you remember to get a gift for the wedding?
B: last / we / present / a / week / them / sent / yeah
____
____

4 A: Where did you get this idea for the wedding invitations from?
B: it / mom / thought / up / my
____
____

5 A: Did you remember to get in touch with everybody about his or her dietary requirements for the wedding?
B: an / I'll / them / email / send / right away
____
____

6 A: How was the food tasting for the wedding?
B: food / the / prepared / beautifully / caterers / the / absolutely
____
____

C Make it personal Complete the sentences so they're true for you.

1 When I need to think things over, I usually ________________________________.
2 When I have to make small talk, I usually ________________________________.
3 The best place/time to think up new ideas is ________________________________.

9.2 What behavior is rude in your culture?

A Look at the photo and think of two things you should and shouldn't do when in Dubai. Read the text to check your ideas.

B 35 Complete the tips with non-restrictive clauses (1–6). Listen to check.

1 which is why the malls are a top destination for visitors.
2 which makes it uncomfortable to be out at any time of day.
3 which means you'll probably visit it at some point if you're a business traveler.
4 which is a perfect time to meet local people as well as try the local cuisine.
5 which is one place where beach wear is acceptable.
6 which will make you feel like you're in a science-fiction movie!

Dos and Don'ts – Dubai, United Arab Emirates

Dubai, a city in the desert, is rapidly becoming a major transportation hub, [A] ________ . Whether there on a stopover, a vacation, or for business, here are five tips to make the most of the city.

Do

- Visit the Burj Khalifa. It's the world's tallest building made of glass and steel, [B] ________ .
- Go shopping. Shopping is a national pastime in Dubai, [C] ________ . They are like cities in themselves. They contain vending machines that sell gold, as well as artificial ski slopes, and giant aquariums.
- Accept any invitation to an *ifta* meal during Ramadan. People don't eat during the day during this religious festival, but they have a feast in the evening at sunset, [D] ________ .

Don't

- Visit in July or August, if at all possible. The weather is incredibly hot and humid, [E] ________ .
- Wear revealing clothing. Both men and women in the gulf wear long sleeves and cover their legs. The exception is at the city's beautiful beaches, [F] ________ .

C Cross out the extra word in each sentence.

1 My sister is always borrowing my clothes, which that gets on my nerves.
2 Nobody writes "dear" or even "hello" in emails any more, which I think it is really rude.
3 Kimchi, which I love it, is the spicy national dish of Korea.
4 The best time to visit my country is spring, when which it is warm and sunny.
5 The Lemon Tree Restaurant, which where we personally recommend, has amazing desserts.
6 Arriving late for class or meetings, which is common in my country, it is considered rude in Japan.

D Make it personal Complete the advice for your country.

1 The best time to visit my country is ________________ , which ________________________________ .
2 Our national dish is ________________ , which ________________________________ .
3 One thing to avoid in my country is ________________ , which ________________________________ .

A It's a myth that only teenagers feel stressed by social media. People of all ages feel under tremendous pressure to keep up to date with Twitter, Facebook, and the rest. Thankfully, there are ways to reduce this level of stress.

B First of all, keep it small. Having lots of friends and followers gives you a massive egoboo (an 'ego boost') in the beginning, but it soon becomes difficult to keep responding to all those messages you receive from people you barely know. Only keep in contact with real friends online.

C Users on websites like Facebook create an image where everyone looks prosperous and happy. This makes people feel jealous of others. To avoid this, try not to compare your life to that of your friends and acquaintances online. Just use social media accounts to pass on updates about what's happening in your life.

D Many people also wrongly feel they should be connected to the workplace 24/7. With smartphones, workers can receive emails and WhatsApp messages even when they're not working. In your free time, close the programs and apps that your colleagues use, and don't look at them when you're not at work.

E Another problem in the workplace or at college is multitasking. In any modern classroom, the students have their tablets or laptops on while they listen to the lecturer. As well as taking notes, they check email, write reports, update Twitter, and peek at Facebook. This is too much for the brain to handle and encourages stress. To combat this, try to concentrate on just one task at a time to stop that feeling of a loss of control.

F You cannot control the Internet, but you can reduce the impact of the Internet and social media on your life. Just a few lifestyle changes can help reduce that feeling of stress, which can all too quickly take control of your life.

A Read the article. Choose the best title (1–3).

1 How to use the Internet efficiently at school and at work
2 How the Internet is changing our interests and behavior
3 How to stop teenagers worrying about the online world

B Match summary sentences 1–6 to the paragraphs (A–F).

1 People pretend their lives are perfect when they're on social media. ☐
2 Don't do too many things at once. ☐
3 It's not only young people who feel worried by the online world. ☐
4 Simple changes can make a big difference. ☐
5 It's impossible to stay in touch with everybody. ☐
6 Make sure you disconnect from your office when you're not there. ☐

C Circle the correct alternatives.

1 I *value / worth* my family and relations. They're incredibly important to me.
2 He has a different *appearance / outlook* to me on our career prospects. I'm positive about the future.
3 I couldn't care *less / more* about the changes at our college. They don't interest me at all.
4 People here are very *relaxed / tolerant* of others because there are so many different nationalities living and working together in the same place.
5 Are you *over / under* the impression that we have an exam tomorrow? It's not true if that's what you're thinking.
6 My dad and I don't see eye *to / with* eye about my career path. He wants me to be a lawyer, but I want to study drama.
7 I wasn't *awake / aware* of any disagreements between the teaching assistant and the students when I took the course last month.

D **Make it personal** Re-read 1–7 in **C**. Check (✓) the ones that sound most like something you've said or heard recently.

Would you be a good detective?

A 36 Listen to a news story. Then order the pictures 1–5.

a ☐

b ☐

c ☐

d ☐

e ☐

B 36 Listen again and correct seven more factual errors in this summary of the crime.

A man broke into ~~an apartment~~ *a house* and committed a robbery in Miami. Unfortunately for him, he accidentally left his cell phone behind on a sofa. While the police were investigating the crime scene, his brother called his cell phone, and the police answered it. Not realizing who he was speaking to, he told the police his name because he wanted the phone back. The burglar denied committing the crime, saying that his phone had been lost. However, the police analyzed the messages on the phone and linked the man to four other crimes in the area.

C Reduce the relative clauses in sentences 1–7.

1 A man ~~who was~~ walking his dog witnessed the burglar leaving the property.
2 I get really annoyed at these companies who are calling my phone.
3 The man who was seen near the crime scene was wearing a red jacket.
4 Anyone who requires a special meal should reserve one online before the flight.
5 Books which are returned late to the library will incur a fine of 50 cents a day.
6 Only food that has been bought in the cafeteria may be eaten at these tables.
7 People who arrive late will not be admitted to the theater.

D Cross out the word which is different from the others in each group.

1 arrest burgle steal rob
2 burglar suspect robber thief
3 accept admit agree deny
4 rub scratch nod touch
5 invent comment lie make up
6 cheat allow litter speed

A problem-solution essay

A Choose the correct alternatives to complete the essay.

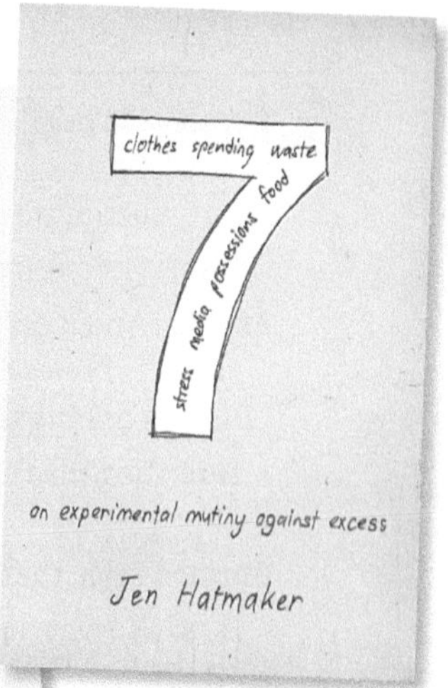

What to do with all this clutter?

We are a nation of shopaholics. We buy more and more things that we don't need [1]*as / despite* more and more of our free time is spent in the mall. The problem comes when we take it all home. [2]*Although / Unlike* people in the countryside, we city dwellers have no room in our small apartments for all these new purchases. Our homes are full of clutter.

Author Jen Hatmaker proposes an interesting solution. In her book *7: An experimental mutiny against excess*, Hatmaker says we should follow the rule of seven [3]*because / in order to* reduce our spending. For example, she only wore seven items of clothing for a whole month [4]*despite / so* that having a closet full of them. Even more surprisingly, she only ate seven types of food for a month, too.

[5]*As / Due to* the discovery that she had hundreds of pants, tops, and skirts that she didn't need, Hatmaker decided to clear out her closet. She gave these excess items away to charity [6]*although / so that* other people could use them. Suddenly, she had no clutter.

[7]*Due to / While* most of us could only dream of having a closet like that, there are other simple ways of doing something similar. For example, you could cook the same seven meals each week [8]*because / in order to* then you know exactly how much food to buy each time you go to the store.

[9]*Although / Unlike* Hatmaker's approach may seem too extreme for most people to follow, she does have powerful arguments for cutting down on all the clutter in our lives.

B T (true) or F (false)? We can infer that the author of the essay ...

1 is a shopaholic.
2 has a large house.
3 has hundreds of clothes.
4 doesn't often have enough money to eat well.
5 agrees with some, but not all, of Hatmaker's ideas.

C Correct the mistake in each sentence.

1 Not like my brother who speaks French and Chinese, I'm terrible at languages. ______________
2 I wasn't able to go to the show due to have too much work. ______________
3 You need to pass an English test in order to studying at a college in the U.S. ______________
4 I'll upload the photos to the website so what everyone can see them. ______________
5 Despite it was hot weather, they wouldn't put the air conditioning on. ______________
6 We stopped for something to eat because of we had a few hours to wait for our flight.
____

D Look back at lessons 9.1–9.5 in the Student's Book. Find the connection between the song lines and the content of each lesson.

E 37 Listen to the five question titles from the unit, and record your answers to them. If possible, compare recordings with a classmate.

How do you like to get around town?

A 38 Complete the conversation with the correct form of these phrasal verbs. Listen to check.

dawn on	end up	get away	get through	look forward to	mix up

EDDIE: I'm not 1__________ going to dinner at my uncle's tomorrow. I don't know how I 2__________ the last one. It lasted for hours, and we ate more food at one lunch than I usually eat in a year.

IRIS: I know. It's impossible to 3__________. Once you're in the house, you're trapped!

EDDIE: And it only just 4__________ me on that we're supposed to bring the dessert, and now all the bakeries are closed. I'll probably 5__________ making one myself, and you know how bad my cooking is.

IRIS: Yes, please, anything but that! I still haven't recovered from the cake you made last year when you 6__________ the salt and the sugar.

EDDIE: Yeah, that was one of the worst. Well, I guess, you could cook if you like.

IRIS: No way. It's your family, Eddie – your cake!

B Correct the mistake in each sentence. One sentence is correct.

1 I'm not looking forward to go to the hospital tomorrow. __________
2 It only just dawned me on that we need a visa to go to the U.S. __________
3 That traffic jam was horrendous. Thank goodness, we finally got it through. __________
4 Some guy was painting graffiti right outside our apartment building, but he got away before the police arrived. __________
5 My dad always calls me by my sister's name, and vice-versa. He's always mixing up us. __________

C 39 Listen to Dave's travel nightmare story. Complete the summary.

Dave, who is a 1__________, describes a terrible flight between 2__________ and 3__________. On the flight, a 4__________ suddenly became ill. Dave helped and as a reward, he was given 5__________ tickets to go 6__________ by the airline.

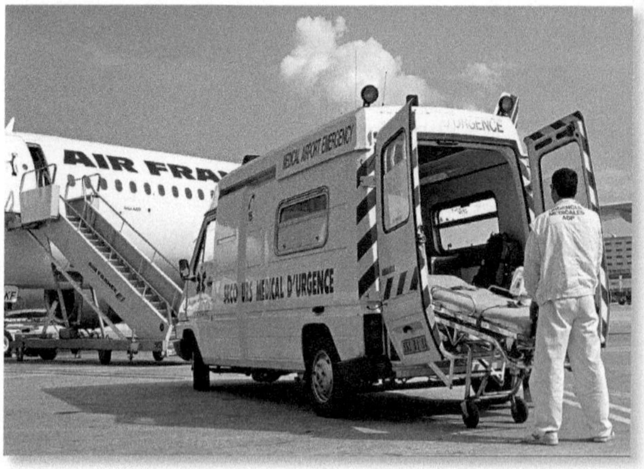

D 39 Listen again. T (true) or F (false)?

1 The other passenger was sitting across from Dave.
2 The man looked pale and was unable to speak.
3 The co-pilot whispered to Dave so nobody could hear them.
4 The man became ill towards the end of the flight.
5 When they landed, the doctor on the ground spoke the man's language.
6 The man made a complete recovery.

E **Make it personal** Complete the sentences so they're true for you.

1 The best way for a tourist to get around my hometown is __________.
2 To get around myself, I usually __________.
3 If I were really rich, my preferred form of transportation would be __________.
4 If I ran out of gas while driving near my home, I'd __________.

A Complete 1–5 with the noun form of these phrasal verbs. There's one extra.

break down	check out	hand out	log in	mix up	rip off

1 I'm afraid there's been a ________________ with your reservation. We'll need to arrange a room for you at another hotel.
2 They charged me $20 for a burger! It was a complete ________________ .
3 We had a ________________ on the highway. The car just stopped, and we couldn't start it again.
4 I can't use the hotel website because I don't have a ________________ or a password.
5 What time is ________________ tomorrow morning? Do I have to leave the hotel before midday?

B 40 Circle the correct alternatives. Listen to check.

CHLOE: While I'm here in Colombia, I'd love to go to your famous mud baths. Could you tell me where [1]*they are / are they*?
PATY: The mud baths? That's my idea of a perfect vacation! Volcanic mud! It's so much fun! They're very near us here in Cartagena. The place is called El Totumo.
CHLOE: Do you know how long [2]*it takes / does it take* to get there?
PATY: Not long. It's only 45 minutes from the city center.
CHLOE: Do you happen [3]*know / to know* if they speak English there?
PATY: Yes, no problem. Lots of people speak English at the baths.
CHLOE: Oh, and I'd like to know [4]*whether / which* I can bring my own food. We want to have a picnic.
PATY: That's fine. In fact, you have to bring your own food. There isn't a restaurant or café there.
CHLOE: One more thing. Can you check if [5]*it is open / is it open* tomorrow?
PATY Let me see. Just checking now. Er, yes, that's fine. It's open.
CHLOE: Wow, great! I'm going. One last thing: I wonder how [6]*do I get / I get* the mud off afterwards.
PATY: That's the really fun part. You wash it off in the river next to the volcano!
CHLOE: No way!
PATY: Yes, absolutely. Everybody does it. You'll love it!

C Order the words to make questions.

1 is / like / summer / to / whether / know / I'd / in / your / country / very hot

____

2 what time / you / me / could / most stores / tell / in / city / your capital / open / ?

____

3 your / of / know / home / the name / a good restaurant / happen to / you / near / do / ?

____

D **Make it personal** Answer the questions in **C** so they're true for you.

1 ____
2 ____
3 ____

Reflections on my time in Japan

Elma Pereira

I went to Japan last year, and I fell in love with the country. Coming from São Paulo, it was a real culture shock at first, but it was also a homecoming for me. My grandparents emigrated to Brazil from Japan 50 years ago, and it was my first time going back to their homeland. I was discovering my **roots**. Now I'm thinking of studying there for a while.

The food was a real highlight for me. Everyone knows sushi, but I also loved the traditional noodles. You dip them into a kind of hot broth, which is like soup. They often come with bits of fish, which you **crumble** into soy sauce to make it tastier. There's nothing better on a frosty winter's day.

In Brazil, I'm studying fashion and I want to design clothes for a living. One of the great things about Tokyo's shops is that many sell beautiful fabrics. People buy these to make kimonos and other traditional garments. I bought so many samples from these shops, and they often don't even have a **label**. I'm now bursting with ideas for new designs.

Moving to Japan would be a big **leap** for me. One thing that will make the transition easier is that people are so friendly. People helped me out everywhere, and often spoke English, which was great because I could only say "arigato" and "sayonara" and you can't get far saying "thank you" and "good bye"!

I stayed at my cousins' house, which was a great way not only to save money – as accommodation and eating out are very expensive – but also to see how ordinary people live. Their apartment was very small, much smaller than ours back in Brazil, but it was brilliantly designed. Everything **fit** in a particular place, so you never noticed how small the living space actually was.

For me, the clothes in Japan are a **magnet** that draws me in and makes me want to learn more about the country. That's really why I want to live there, to learn how to capture the spirit of Japanese design.

A Read Elma's blog post. Check (✓) the things that she mentions.

☐ famous places ☐ clothes ☐ hotels ☐ meals ☐ parks ☐ the cost of living
☐ public transportation ☐ weather ☐ useful phrases ☐ people's homes ☐ the character of the people

B Re-read the blog. T (true) or F (false)?

1 Elma's parents originally come from Japan.
2 A broth is a liquid.
3 Elma is only interested in brand-name products.
4 She found it impossible to communicate with people.
5 She saw some relatives while she was in Tokyo.
6 She wants to get a job in Japan in the future.

C Do the words in bold in the blog have a literal (L) or figurative (F) meaning?

1 roots ☐ 2 crumble ☐ 3 label ☐ 4 leap ☐ 5 fit ☐ 6 magnet ☐

D **Make it personal** Complete the sentence so it's true for you.

I would / wouldn't like to live in Japan because ______________________________.

A 41 Complete the instant message conversation with these words. There's one extra. Listen to check.

barely	culture clash	here and there	homesick	hustle and bustle	let alone	overwhelming

Hey Sis!

Hi! How's your new life in Rome?

Amazing! The [1]__________ of the city is great – I love getting lost in the crowds.

Cool! Do you miss home?

No, I don't feel [2]__________ at all! Maybe it's because of all the history. It's quite [3]__________. People have been walking these streets for over 2,000 years!

Amazing! But what's everyday life like?

I've only had one [4]__________ so far. There are no supermarkets in my local area, [5]__________ a department store. That means I have to ask for products when I go shopping because everything is behind the counter.

Oh no! And you can [6]__________ say anything more than "pizza" or "spaghetti" in Italian!

That's right! So as you can imagine, I've been eating a lot of pasta!

B Circle the correct alternatives.

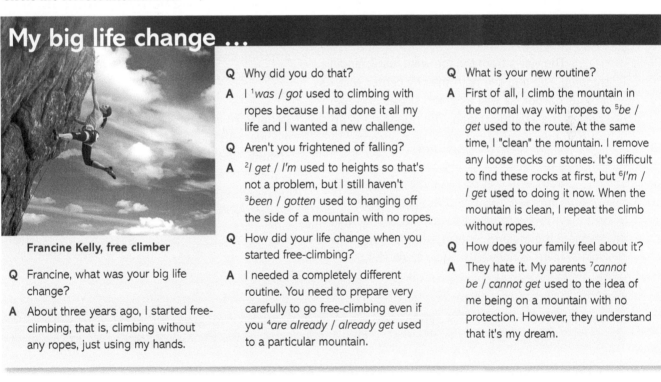

My big life change ...

Francine Kelly, free climber

Q Francine, what was your big life change?

A About three years ago, I started free-climbing, that is, climbing without any ropes, just using my hands.

Q Why did you do that?

A I [1]*was / got* used to climbing with ropes because I had done it all my life and I wanted a new challenge.

Q Aren't you frightened of falling?

A [2]*I get / I'm* used to heights so that's not a problem, but I still haven't [3]*been / gotten* used to hanging off the side of a mountain with no ropes.

Q How did your life change when you started free-climbing?

A I needed a completely different routine. You need to prepare very carefully to go free-climbing even if you [4]*are already / already get* used to a particular mountain.

Q What is your new routine?

A First of all, I climb the mountain in the normal way with ropes to [5]*be / get* used to the route. At the same time, I "clean" the mountain. I remove any loose rocks or stones. It's difficult to find these rocks at first, but [6]*I'm / I get* used to doing it now. When the mountain is clean, I repeat the climb without ropes.

Q How does your family feel about it?

A They hate it. My parents [7]*cannot be / cannot get* used to the idea of me being on a mountain with no protection. However, they understand that it's my dream.

C Correct the mistake in each sentence. One sentence is correct.

1 Novak's working nights on his new job. He doesn't like it, but he's slowly used to it. __________

2 Living in Moscow is great, but we can't got used to cold weather. __________

3 Alexis was angry because the train was an hour late, but I'm used to train delays so it wasn't a problem for me. __________

4 I can't be used to being the project leader. I feel uncomfortable telling people what to do. __________

5 They say you get use to getting up at 5 a.m., but you never do. __________

6 If you need someone to drive the van for the trip, I can do it. I drive one for work, so I get used to it. __________

Which are your two favorite cities and why?

A travel report

A Circle the correct alternatives (1–7) to complete the travel report below.

B ▶42 Re-read and complete paragraphs a–f with topic sentences 1–6. Listen to check.

1 Table Mountain sits above the city, and it's an iconic image of Cape Town.
2 If that wasn't enough, Cape Town also serves as a handy base for wildlife watching.
3 Cape Town is one of the most spectacular cities in the world, not just in South Africa.
4 By contrast, Robben Island is a tragic reminder of our country's difficult past.
5 The city has a Mediterranean climate, so it's pleasant to visit all year round.
6 Back at street level, you can explore the city's wide range of architectural styles.

The Cape of Good Times   Alexandra Biko

a______ I went there for the first time this year from my home town of Johannesburg, and it [1]*blew / broke* me away. Cape Town will [2]*put / set* your imagination on fire.

b______ It can be wet in winter and quite windy, too. The best time to visit is March through May, when the weather is perfect.

c______ The views from the top were just [3]*standing / stunning*. You can see both the city center with its famous harbor, as well as green slopes and the coast of the Atlantic Ocean. The ride there is epic, too. You take a cable car from the city center to the summit.

d______ Start with a stroll around the old town. Many of the buildings here are over 300 years old, and they have a range of colonial styles. Nearby is Bo-Kaap, the Muslim District, with its [4]*gorgeous / grateful* town houses and exotic spice shops.

e______ It was the prison where many people were once incarcerated. Nelson Mandela was one of the most famous prisoners there. The story of his struggle is [5]*awe-inspiring / good-looking*.

f______ It's not really safari territory, but you can go to the whale coast, one of the best places in the world to see right whales. The sight of these amazing creatures will [6]*put / take* your breath away, and it's just 115 kilometers from the city center.

Cape Town is magnificent. The culture, history, wildlife, and friendly people make it a trip of a lifetime. Watching dawn rise over Table Mountain is a sight that is magnificent [7]*above / beyond* your wildest dreams. It's a perfect location for a vacation.

C **Make it personal** Imagine you want to visit Cape Town. Write a comment to post at the end of Alexandra's travel report. Include one question you could ask her.

____

____

D Look back at lessons 10.1–10.5 in the Student's Book. Find the connection between the song lines and the content of each lesson.

E ▶43 Listen to the five question titles from this unit, and record your answers to them. If possible, compare recordings with a classmate.

1 » 11.1 What recent news has caught your eye?

A 44 Listen and match the news stories 1–5 to the categories. There are two extra categories.

☐ Arts ☐ Crime ☐ Eating out ☐ Education ☐ Property ☐ Sports ☐ Unemployment

B 44 Listen again. Correct two pieces of false information in each summary.

News | Sport | Weather | Entertainment

1 ~~Argentinian~~ Brazilian Paulo Orlando has become the first player from his country to play in the Baseball World Series. His team, the Kansas City Royals, lost the series against the New York Mets 4–1.

2 Some families in the U.S. are paid to live in empty homes. They don't have to clean it, but they do have to stay in the house because people are more likely to buy a property if someone lives there. The family members must always be at home when people come to see the property.

3 Mallie's Sports Bar and Grill in Northgate, Michigan, makes the world's largest burger. It weighs around 150 kilos, and you have to order it the day before you eat it.

4 The stars of Russia's Bolshoi Ballet are frequent visitors to Canada, and this year's tour features performances of the *Nutcracker* in Toronto and *Don Quixote* in Ottawa.

5 Oklahoma University Professor Kieran Mullen made headlines by destroying a laptop in front of his class. He picked up the machine from a desk and placed it in liquid oxygen, then dropped it on the floor where it broke into two halves. Fortunately, it was all a hoax designed to make his students concentrate on the class and not their computer screens.

C Complete the comments on a newspaper's website with these phrases.

an accurate source	behind-the-scenes	biased	caught my eye	keep up with	skip

1 Your sports correspondent is ________ against my team. He's always criticizing the New England Patriots. He doesn't have a good word to say about them.
2 It's easy for your newspaper to criticize the president, but you don't know what's happening ________. She has access to information that none of your correspondents has.
3 It's crazy to use comments from a blogger to say that vaccinations are not safe. That blog was not ________ of information. It was written neither by a doctor nor a scientist.
4 I'm very disappointed you're no longer running reviews of Broadway plays. I subscribe to your paper just to ________ what's happening in the theater. Now, I'll be forced to look elsewhere.
5 A photo in your world news section ________ last weekend. Although the caption read that it was the Prime Minister of the Republic of Ireland, it was actually the country's President.
6 Like most people, I usually ________ the business pages, but I happened to read Maggie Bigelow's article on the Ivory Coast last weekend, and I found it fascinating. Congratulations!

D **Make it personal** Complete the sentences so they're true for you.

1 I don't read all of the news online. I usually skip ________.
2 One website I always look at it is ________ to keep up with news about ________.
3 The last photo that caught my eye was one of ________.

A Complete the phrases to describe being relaxed or nervous.

Have you ever laughed at the wrong moment?

Oh yes, absolutely, and my roommate, Rodrigo, was so angry – he completely [1]l______________ it. It all happened last year. Rodrigo was going away for the week, so I decided to earn a bit of extra money by renting out our apartment online to some tourists. I figured Rodrigo would be away so he would never see them. Boy oh boy, I was so wrong!

It was around the time when that volcano erupted here in Chile, and all flights were canceled. So without me knowing, Rodrigo had to come back to the apartment. He was in the shower when my guests, this family of four, entered the apartment. He completely [2]f______________ out. Luckily, the family kept their [3]c______________. The mother called my cell phone, and I explained the mix-up.

I asked her to stay [4]c______________ and pass the phone to Rodrigo. He was still in the living room in his robe! Well, I couldn't keep it [5]t______________ any longer, and I just started to laugh. He went ballistic. Not surprisingly, we stopped sharing a place soon after that! Oh, and the family never paid me a cent, either, as they ended up staying at a hotel.

B Report sentences 1–6 from the story. Remember to move the verb one tense back.

1 "There are some strangers in our apartment!"
Rodrigo said ______________________________.

2 "No flights were able to leave today because of the volcano."
Rodrigo said ______________________________.

3 "We booked the apartment online."
The mother said ______________________________.

4 "We can always stay at a hotel."
The father said ______________________________.

5 "I'll never forgive you for this!"
Rodrigo said ______________________________.

6 "I'm really, really sorry, Rodrigo."
I told Rodrigo ______________________________.

C Put the words in order to complete the reported questions.

1 (there / they / doing / were / what) Rodrigo asked the family ______________________.

2 (I / when / back / was / coming) Rodrigo asked ______________________.

3 (mistake / whether / a / there / had / been) The mother asked ______________________.

4 (go / would / where / they) We asked the family ______________________.

A 45 Read the article and put the paragraphs A–E in order 1–5. Listen to check.

The Dancing Traffic Light Manikin

A ☐ By waiting and watching the movements of this figure, these people aren't trying to rush across the road. As the video says, pedestrian crossings are the most dangerous place for traffic accidents in cities. By contrast, the green figure just stands still. Otherwise people would watch it dancing, too!

B ☐ This is what led to its huge viral success. It has, count them, over 115 million views on YouTube. In addition, 81% more people waited at the light, avoiding any possibility of accidents. That's something to be proud of.

C 1 People falling over, cats in hats, celebrity jokes: there are lots of reasons why a video might go viral, but surely the best of all is because it saves lives. That was the case in the 2014 hit *The Dancing Traffic Light Manikin* by Smart.

D ☐ Haven't seen it? The idea is simple. Pedestrians wait at a busy pedestrian crossing. The red figure tells them to stop, but instead of standing in one place, it starts to dance in lots of different ways. The people waiting start laughing, and watch the red figure dancing until the end.

E ☐ But just waiting at the traffic light wouldn't make the video go viral: there's also a catch. The dancing traffic light isn't pre-programmed. It imitates live dancing by members of the public. People go into a special booth where a camera records their dance steps. These are then copied by the red figure on the traffic light.

B Re-read. T (true), F (false) or NI (no information)? Have you seen the video? If not, search for it online.

1 The Dancing Light Manikin was set up in lots of different cities.
2 The objective of the video was to encourage public safety.
3 81% of all pedestrians waited to watch the video.
4 Almost all viral videos are funny ones.
5 Only the red figure moves in the traffic light.
6 The red man copies the movements of professional dancers.

C Match 1–6 to responses a–f.

1 I didn't know that most road accidents happen at pedestrian crossings.
2 I saw a video of a grandfather seeing his grandson for the first time after 25 years.
3 This hip-hop video is so cool. I've been dancing to it all week.
4 I can't believe you were on the news. I thought you were far too shy to talk to a reporter.
5 Did you see that video of the wedding group on a bridge, where the bridge breaks and they all fall into the water?
6 I really hate videos where people are cruel to animals.

a ☐ I agree. That gets to me, too.
b ☐ Really? It does nothing for me.
c ☐ Me too. It moved me to tears.
d ☐ No. That got me thinking, too.
e ☐ Oh yeah! I burst out laughing.
f ☐ What can I say? They caught me by surprise.

What's your definition of gossip?

A 46 Complete the conversations with these phrases. Listen to check.

between you and me	didn't tell a soul	have my word	keep it to yourself
me and my big mouth	my lips are sealed	never guess	spread it around

Conversation 1

A: There's only one way that Karen found out about the surprise party. You told her.

B: No! I swear! I [1]________________ !

A: Well, anyway, she knows now. Just don't tell Daisy too, all right?

B: She won't hear about it from me. [2]________________ .

A: She'd better not. I'm just worried that Mike is going to [3]________________ . That guy can't keep a secret to save his life.

B: Trust me, OK. He won't say anything. You [4]________________ .

A: You'd better be right!

Conversation 2

C: I heard that your brother was caught cheating on an exam.

D: Yes, well, no one else knows, so [5]________________ , OK?

C: Oh! I told Nigel, too.

D: What?

C: [6]________________ . I'm so sorry. We were talking about the exam, and it slipped out.

D: Well, please, please don't tell anyone else.

C: OK but, [7]________________ , he wasn't the only one they caught cheating. You'll [8]________________ who else was caught. Michael Parker!

D: No way!

C: Yes! Ah, you like hearing about secrets now.

B Correct the mistake in each sentence. One sentence is correct.

1 The doctor urged me do more exercise for the sake of my health. ________________
2 They agreed no to tell anyone the news until Monday. ________________
3 Bill promised help me find a job as soon as possible. ________________
4 My parents persuaded me go to college. I didn't want to go. ________________
5 They threatened throwing us off the train if we didn't show them our tickets. ________________
6 Hugo's parents begged him not to join the fire department because they thought it was too dangerous. ________________
7 The hotel refused refund my money even though I showed them that I had overpaid. ________________
8 I wanted to talk about our Internet site in the meeting, but they wouldn't let me to change the subject. ________________

C Choose the correct alternatives. Have you ever played *Telephone*? What's it called in your language?

We've all played the game *Telephone*. In this simple game, you stand in line. The person at one end thinks of a sentence. He or she whispers it in a neighbor's ear and tells that person [1]*repeat / to repeat* the sentence to a neighbor, and so on until everyone has heard and repeated it. Everyone then compares the final sentence with the original to see whether or not it's the same. The person who came up with the sentence has to promise [2]*not to tell / to not tell* it to anyone until the end.

In 2012, an Australian man called Philip Minchin persuaded people all around the world [3]*joining / to join* a global game of *Telephone*. People in libraries all over the world agreed [4]*to play / play*. They even let people [5]*take part / to take part* whose first language wasn't English. It began in Melbourne, Australia as "Life must be lived as play," a quotation from the Greek Philosopher Plato. The message then moved across six continents until it reached Alaska, in the U.S. And the final message? Nobody expected [6]*hearing / to hear* the same sentence, but what was repeated was completely bizarre: "He bites snails!"

A letter of complaint

A Read the email and check (✓) the four items that Silvio complains about.

1 ☐ the availability of seats
2 ☐ the in-flight menu
3 ☐ his luggage
4 ☐ the company website
5 ☐ the staff
6 ☐ the cost of the tickets

To: customerservices@flyways.net
From: sbacelli@mymail.net
Subject: Complaint

Dear Sir / Madam

I am writing to you in [1]r__ g__ __ __ to my experience on flight XL923 with your airline on August 9th. I had booked three seats on this flight for myself and my parents. Our experience was extremely unsatisfactory, so I am writing to complain.

First of all, our flight was overbooked, and only two people were allowed to board. We were obviously unwilling to split our group, so we were all forced to wait for the next flight. This overbooking took place despite the fact that we had previously reserved seats online.

It is my [2]b__ __ __ __f that we are entitled to compensation as a result of the long wait in the airport, during which we were only given a $5 voucher for some sandwiches.

To make [3]m__ __t __ __s worse, before we boarded the later flight, we were asked to place our bags in the hold. Your unsympathetic staff insisted very forcefully that our bags were too large to go in the overhead compartments in the cabin. Your website claims that passengers are permitted to carry bags of 25x45x56 centimeters on all flights. In [4]r__ __ l__ __y, bags of that size are only permitted for business class customers. Your website is misleading.

I would also like to [5]c__ __ __ your attention to the government guidelines for fair treatment of passengers. Following the information given there, I believe that we are entitled to a refund on the price of our tickets for this flight.

Sincerely

Silvio Bacelli

B Complete the missing letters in the phrases for writing a letter or email of complaint.

C Silvio also ordered a special vegetarian meal for the flight. This was forgotten, and he was only offered a standard meal. Add this complaint to his email.

____

____

D Look back at lessons 11.1–11.5 in the Student's Book. Find the connection between the song lines and the content of each lesson.

E ▶47 Listen to the five question titles from the unit, and record your answers to them. If possible, compare recordings with a classmate.

How optimistic are you?

A ▶48 Read the podcast title. Guess if the speakers will agree (A) or disagree (D) with these statements. Listen to check your ideas.

1 Optimists often make mistakes with money.
2 Pessimists make bad employees.
3 Pessimists are better at planning than optimists.
4 Optimists are healthier people than pessimists.
5 Pessimists tend to take lots of safety precautions.

Today on the podcast: "It's not all bad" – why a little bit of pessimism can be good for you, with Jenna Doyle and Keith Woods.

B ▶48 Listen again and complete the summary with words you hear on the podcast.

People think pessimism is bad, a destructive form of [1]____________, but, in fact, it can be a good thing. Optimists often [2]____________ a lot of money because they are sure that they can pay it back, which is not always true.

Pessimists are also more effective in the workplace. Although people are expected to be positive in [3]____________, in working life, pessimists are better because they make better [4]____________ for the future.

Surprisingly, [5]____________ doctors have found that pessimism is also good for health. Pessimists go to the doctor as soon as possible, whereas optimists often [6]____________ medical problems until it's too late. In the same way, pessimists are less likely to be injured in accidents because they take [7]____________ precautions like wearing a helmet on a bike.

Being a pessimist is not [8]____________ – there are benefits to looking on the bad side of life.

C Complete the conversations with these words. There are two extras.

best	better	bright	dream	good	safe	tunnel	wishful

1 A: I have my lottery ticket, and we're going to be millionaires on Friday!
B: Yeah, ____________ on!

2 A: I went for a job interview on Monday, and they still haven't gotten back to me.
B: Don't worry. No news is ____________ news.

3 A: If we hang around outside the movie opening, we might get to take a selfie with one of the stars.
B: Come on, Lucas, that's just ____________ thinking.

4 A: Do we really need to take all these medicines with us on vacation? Your suitcase is like a pharmacy!
B: Better ____________ than sorry.

5 A: I'm worrying it might rain over the weekend, and we're having a barbecue.
B: Yes, but it also might not. You have to hope for the ____________ .

6 A: How frustrating! The office computer system is down. I can't do anything.
B: Well, look on the ____________ side; we can probably go home early today.

A Can you imagine a 3D phone? Read the article and circle the correct alternatives.

The 3D phone is coming

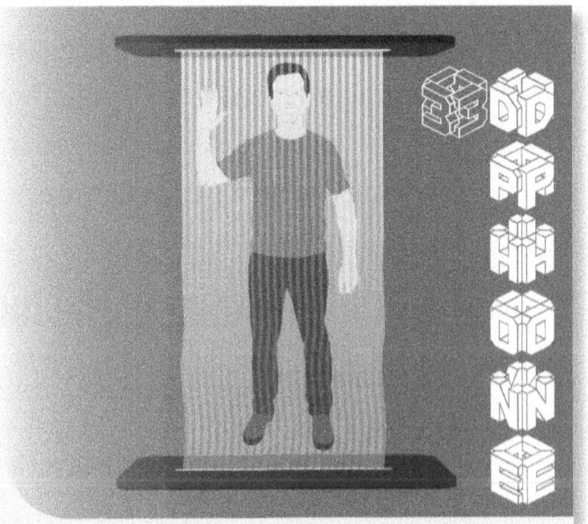

What will future phone calls be like?

Forget video calls. All of us will soon [1]*have made / be making* 3D calls all day, every day. Polish company Leia Display Systems is already building a prototype which will [2]*be completely finishing / have completely finished* by the end of next year. *Star Wars* fans will [3]*have already recognized / already be recognizing* that the company is named after Princess Leia, who sends a 3D hologram of herself in *Star Wars*.

How will the 3D phone [4]*work / be working*?

To send calls, users will [5]*sit / have sat* in front of a special camera, which records their image and sends it to the recipient. Then a laser projects the caller's image onto water vapor, which creates a 3D image of them. Users [6]*will need / be needing* a large room to receive calls because the image is life-size. The developers [7]*have worked / will be working* on a smaller version once the original goes on sale.

Who's the 3D phone for?

Although most of us will [8]*continue / have continued* to use our traditional smartphones, the 3D version has some particularly useful applications. In the first few years, people will probably [9]*be using / have used* it for acting auditions, or in the fashion industry to see how clothes look on models. This [10]*will be saving / is going to save* thousands of dollars in plane fares if customers can appear to be in the same room even if they are actually hundreds of miles away.

B Rewrite the sentences using the word in CAPITALS. Do not change the word.

1 We're going to finish our project before March 4th. HAVE

We'll have finished our project by March 4th.

2 The population will certainly keep growing. BOUND

____

3 This time tomorrow, we're going to be sitting on a beach in Acapulco. WILL

____

4 Everyone will leave before midnight, I promise you. LEFT

____

5 In 2050, people will be living on the surface of Mars. ARE

____

6 Barcelona FC will probably win the League next year. LIKELY

____

C Put *by* in the correct place or places in these sentences.

1 *Hamlet*, which was written Shakespeare in about 1599, remains his best-known play.

2 This cake was made me and my mom – do you want some?

3 We walked here, but are getting home taxi as we have to be home midnight.

4 Bus fares have gone up 10% in the last year and trains even more!

What's the coldest place you've ever been to?

A Read the article and answer the questions.

1 Where is Oymyakon?
2 What was the coldest ever temperature recorded there?
3 How can you translate "Oymyakon" into English?
4 When do public buildings close in Oymyakon?
5 How long does it take to get there from the airport?

The coldest town in the world ... gets even colder!

Temperatures in Oymyakon fell to new lows last night as winter gripped this town in north-western Russia. The mercury dropped to an incredible –71 Centigrade, the lowest figure ever recorded for a populated area.

Set in one of the most hostile environments imaginable and originally a stopover point for farmers to sell their reindeer, farmers were attracted to the town's hot springs, giving Oymyakon its surprising name – it means something like "the water that doesn't freeze."

Winter is inevitably a long, hard time for local residents to endure. Coupled with the problems of ice and snow, there are also frequent communication breakdowns; it's so cold cell phones won't work!

As long-distance travel gets easier, you'd expect residents to leave for places with warmer weather, but it seems locals are used to their tough environment. Life carries on as normally as possible. For example, the local school will remain open as long as it's warmer than –50 Centigrade outside!

Other temperature-related issues Oymyakonians have to deal with include leaving their cars running when not in use because that way they are bound to start when they need them. Sometimes once the engine is turned off, vehicles never work again.

As the world's temperatures get ever more extreme, who knows what the future holds for this desolate community? Perhaps ever more curious visitors will want to explore this northern region where no crops grow, and the only industry is cutting wood. Without a doubt, anyone brave enough to pay Oymyakon a call will be a true adventurer. It is only accessible by snow-covered roads, a two-day trip from the nearest airport at Yakutsk. That's if the planes are running, of course. Feeling brave? Come visit Oymyakon!

B Check (✓) the statements the writer is certain about.

1 Oymyakon is the most hostile urban environment in the world.
2 Cell phones cannot function in Oymyakon in winter.
3 Residents leave their engines running to be sure that the car won't break down.
4 The new low temperatures will bring lots of new tourists to the town.
5 Oymyakon is a tourist destination only for the adventurous.

C Complete the phrases in these exchanges.

1 A: Do you think Dirk will be able to complete the marathon?
B: I h_________ my d_________. He's not in great shape, but you never know.

2 A: Wow, that skateboarding trick was amazing! I've caught it on camera.
B: I know. I can't believe I p_________ it o_________! I've never been able to do it before!

3 A: We have five guests staying tonight, but only two bedrooms. I don't know what to do.
B: Don't worry. We'll f_________ o_________ a way to fit everyone in.

4 A: Something's wrong with my laptop. The screen keeps switching off. Any idea why?
B: Sorry, I don't h_________ a c_________. Guess you need to get it to an expert.

5 A: Have you heard about this new virus? What are they saying in the papers?
B: They say it could p_________ a t_________ to people throughout the region.

A Circle the correct alternatives.

1 A: Could you tell me what time the ferry is?
B: *It always leaves / It's always leaving* at 8 a.m., and then *it comes back / it's coming* back at 5.30 p.m. every day.

2 A: Do you know what you are doing over the weekend?
B: Not sure. I guess *I'll watch / I'm watching* a movie, but I have no idea, really.

3 A: These bags are really heavy. I can't carry them on my own.
B: Really? Wait there! *I'm helping / I'll help* you.

4 A: George! I think *it's raining / it's going to rain*. Can you bring the laundry in, please?
B: What? It's OK. There aren't any clouds out there. Let's leave the clothes out.

5 A: I really need someone to help me move this evening.
B: Really? I *don't do / I'm not doing* anything this evening. I can help.

6 A: Who do you think *will win / is winning* the game tomorrow?
B: The Minnesota Timberwolves! They're the best basketball team around.

B 49 Complete the conversation with a future form of the verbs in parentheses. Sometimes more than one form is possible. Listen to hear the most common forms.

BETH: Hey, Charlie, What time 1 ________ (we / meet) for the party tonight?

CHARLIE: I don't know, Beth. Actually ... I can't come.

BETH: What? Everyone thinks you 2 ________ (come)! What's the problem?

CHARLIE: I have a black eye. A real shiner. It's ridiculous. I banged my head on a sign in my local bus station, and it swung back and hit me in the eye. I 3 ________ (write) an email to complain. I'm just thinking about what to say.

BETH: Come on, it's only a black eye. Yes, it's embarrassing, but you got it in an accident. You can't hide at home. Anyway, Milan 4 ________ (bring) a cake for you. He made it this morning, and it looks amazing.

CHARLIE: I'm sorry. I ... I 5 ________ (call) Milan to apologize, OK? I just can't go out. I've already decided. I 6 ________ (stay) at home.

BETH: Look ... I know. I 7 ________ (come) to your house and have a look. I'm sure it's not as bad as you think. Then we 8 ________ (go) to the party together. You 9 ________ (feel) better if you go there with someone else.

CHARLIE: Really? Well, OK, thanks, Beth. You're so kind. But promise you won't laugh, OK?

C Correct the mistake in each sentence. One sentence is correct.

1 I won't go out until your package will arrive, OK? ________
2 I'm going to visit the Prado Museum before I'll leave Madrid. ________
3 We're staying at home until it stops snowing. ________
4 After you will meet Joe, come and see me, please. ________
5 Dana tells you the time of our train as soon as she knows it. ________
6 When I'll get paid, I'll give you back the $100 I owe you. ________

D **Make it personal** What's the worst excuse you have ever heard? Why did the person make the excuse?

____

____

What will your life be like 10 years from now?

A Read Antonia's email to her future self and circle the correct alternatives.

Hello Antonia!

1 How are you? I do hope you're well! This is my email to myself to read at the end of our English course here in Boston! [1]*Hopefully / Officially*, you'll speak much better English when you read this and be able to spot and correct any errors you've made! It's the first day today, and you're going to learn a lot over the next year.

2 My first piece of advice is to keep in touch with everyone you've met in the course. You've [2]*officially / finally* gotten the chance to meet people from all around the world, and you should [3]*definitely / inevitably* try to stay in touch with as many of them as possible. You may even get the chance to visit them.

3 Secondly, I'd encourage you to take a recognized exam in English now. This is [4]*certainly / finally* the best time to do so because you'll have been studying English a lot over the last eight months, and you may never reach the same level again. It's essential to get a document that [5]*officially / probably* shows your English level, for future employers, for example.

4 After the course and the exams, you're [6]*hopefully / inevitably* going to forget a lot of what you've learned, unless you keep working on your English at home. You should read an article that interests you online every day, listen to as much English as possible, and keep chatting with your ex-classmates, too. That way you'll [7]*eventually / officially* get used to "thinking" in English as a daily habit.

5 I imagine you're [8]*definitely / probably* feeling pretty down now at the thought of leaving the U.S. and all your new friends, but try to think positively. Nothing lasts forever, and you've had a great opportunity that many people never get to enjoy.

Have a safe trip home and bye from the past!

Antonia

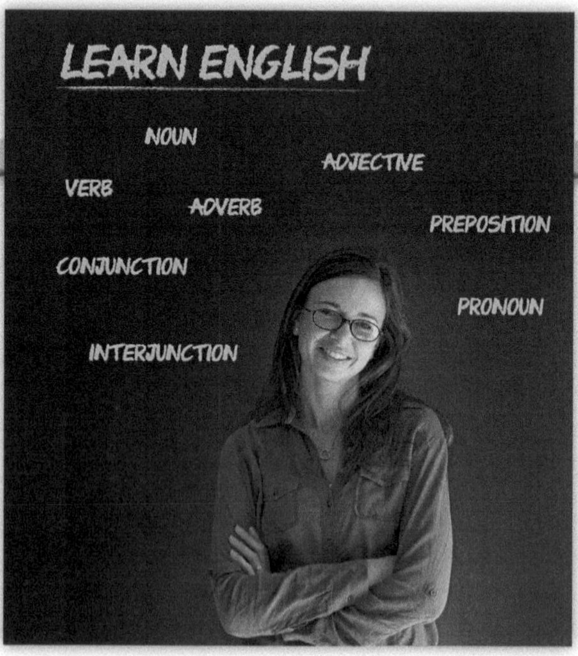

B Re-read and match paragraphs 1–5 to the information they contain. There's one extra.

- ☐ further practice after the course
- ☐ the most important lesson
- ☐ English is important for your career
- ☐ use it as an opportunity to travel
- ☐ when the email was written
- ☐ look on the bright side

C **Make it personal** Look back at a piece of writing you did earlier in the course. What errors can you find? How could you improve it?

D Look back at lessons 12.1–12.5 in the Student's Book. Find the connection between the song lines and the content of each lesson.

E 50 Listen to the five question titles from the unit, and record your answers to them. If possible, compare recordings with a classmate.

28 *page 36 exercises A and B*

J = James Thompson, Y = Adriana Ritchie

J: Adriana, when was the last time you heard kids complaining in an art gallery because they couldn't see enough art?

A: I've never ever heard of that.

J: Don't frown. This really happened.

A: I don't believe you, James. Kids get bored in museums.

J: It happened at the Tate Modern, London's biggest Modern Art gallery.

A: Modern Art? I don't understand that. I spend all my time squinting at the pictures, and I still can't figure out what they are.

J: Tate Modern isn't just about paintings. The museum used to be a power station. Its entrance hall is enormous, and they put giant artworks there. I saw a slide by the Belgian artist Carsten Höller.

A: So the kids were complaining because they couldn't go on the slide?

J: That's right. One of the kids had tickets for the slide, and the others didn't.

A: Uh-oh!

J: It was OK. I had some spare tickets, and I gave them to the kids. We can't let kids miss their favorite art, can we?

A: I'm nodding, listeners, I'm nodding. So how was the slide?

J: It was fun, but it was over in about five seconds. You also had to wear knee pads and elbow pads.

A: What, like on a skateboard? Was it dangerous?

J: No! They were just being careful. Anyway, I wanted another try at it, but the other people with me wanted to see the rest of the gallery, so there wasn't time.

A: OK. I'm scratching my head here, James. How is this slide art?

J: Höller believes that slides are interesting because you lose control on the slide, and you feel really happy afterwards.

A: That's fun, not art.

J: When kids paint, they make art and they have fun.

A: I don't think it's art.

J: Höller also says the slide is an interesting shape. It's round. It has curves. Most of our modern buildings are square, or rectangular. The slide is a different shape. It's another way of looking at the world.

A: Ah, now I understand!

J: You see. Art is for everyone.

A: Can I still see this artwork at the Tate Modern?

J: Sorry, Adriana. It was only a temporary exhibition. Höller's slides have appeared in some other galleries, in Germany and the U.S., so maybe you will see another one somewhere else in the future.

31 *page 39 exercises A and B*

L = Luca, M = Martina

L: Wow! Love the photo, Martina. What a stunning island! Where on earth ...?

M: That, Luca, is Niihau Island in Hawaii.

L: Niihau. I thought that meant Hello in Chinese!

M: Not Nihao. Niihau.

L: Sorry. I've never heard of it!

M: That's because it's one of the most difficult places in the world to visit. For many years, tourists couldn't go to Niihau at all.

L: Why?

M: It's a private island with just a few villages. The owner made the rules. In the past you could only go there if you lived there.

L: But now anyone can go there? Er, are you telling me you were able to visit this place?

M: Uh-huh. Only a few tourists can get in every year. I managed to go there by helicopter with my parents. It was amazing.

L: Lucky you! What's it like? I mean, were you able to meet any of the locals?

M: Yes, one or two. Everyone speaks English. They were very friendly and seemed extremely happy to live in their simple, beautiful island paradise.

L: Awesome! Could you stay the night there?

M: No, our limit was three hours! But at least we were able to go snorkeling. I saw some amazing fish. The sea is crystal clear. And so warm, like the perfect bath! And the beaches are the most wonderful white sand, like walking on warm snow! And ...

L: Stop! I hate you! Did you see any whales or dolphins?

M: No, that's about the only thing we didn't see.

L: Well, I saw a whale once in Mexico. Briefly. Just for a few seconds. I was just able to take a photo before it disappeared under the water.

M: Wow, that's cool.

L: So, do you think I could go to Niihau one day?

M: I don't know. It's not so easy. I mean there are only a few trips every year.

L: But you were able to do it ...

M: That's right but I don't think I could have done it on my own. My parents paid for me to go there. It was very expensive.

L: I can imagine. Wow. I cannot believe that you got to visit your very own desert island.

M: Me neither. Feels like a bit of a dream now, but it was the most amazing experience of my life.

36 *page 46 exercises A and B*

N = News anchor, C = Correspondent

N: OK, next up on the show we have a bizarre true crime story from the Florida area. Our Miami correspondent Clarence Miller is here to tell us all about it. Clarence.

C: Well, Amy, this is really an incredible story. You're going find it very hard to believe! Last week a Florida man, Bradley Philips, was arrested for burglary after calling the police.

N: Back up a minute. The guy was the burglar, and he called the police?

C: That's right.

N: Whoa! How did that happen? Did he have a fight with his partner?

C: No, he committed the crime alone. What happened was that, while Philips was burgling the Miami address, he dropped his cellphone.

N: You mean he left his phone behind in the house?

C: Exactly. The police arrived at the house to investigate the burglary. Suddenly, they heard a phone ringing. They looked around until they found a cellphone on the bed.

N: Did the officers answer the call?

C: You bet they did! They asked who was calling and Philips gave them his address and asked the police to return his phone.

N: So the police went to his house, grabbed him and Philips confessed to his crime?

C: Not at all. When the police accused Philips of burglary, he denied it. Absolutely. He insisted that his phone had been stolen.

N: Was he telling the truth?

C: Absolutely not. He totally made the story up. What gave him away was the fact that the owner of the house had seen him leaving the property.

N: So someone saw him do it?

C: That's right and what's more, the police took fingerprints from his phone and linked those prints to five more burglaries in the area.

N: So then did he own up?

C: No! When Philips went to court, he kept on lying. He still said his phone had been stolen and he denied that anyone saw him near the scene of the burglary.

N: That is astonishing.

C: You're telling me. The crime of the century it was not.

39 *page 48 exercises C and D*

D = Dave, S = Sharon

D: That's just awful. Well, my worst travel experience ever was a flight last year from Japan to France.

S: Yeah? What happened?

D: The man in the seat next to me had a very red face and he was sweating a lot. I mean, his shirt was wet. It turned out that he was having a heart attack.

S: Oh, my goodness. And you're a doctor!

D: Yes. I happened to be in the right place at the right time. He was Japanese and he didn't speak much English so I just diagnozed what was happening. So I started performing first aid when the co-pilot came to speak to me. He said in a loud voice "Do you want me to make an emergency landing?" Everybody on the plane looked at me in silence. For whatever reason, the man said "no, no", and he held my hand, so I thought he was not in immediate danger. As luck would have it, we were very near our final destination so I said we should carry on.

S: What a responsibility.

D: In the end, we arrived in Paris and an ambulance team came on the plane. The local doctor was French but strangely enough she spoke Japanese and she took control of the situation.

S: Astonishing.

D: Yeah. Anyway, in the end, the passenger survived, though he hasn't been allowed to travel again. I think he's in a wheelchair now.

S: Does he communicate with you?

D: Not regularly, but he did send me a beautiful thank you letter. And, the airline gave me two free first-class tickets to go anywhere in the world to say thank you.

S: I think you deserved them!

44 *page 53 exercises A and B*

1 Baseball. Paulo Orlando has made headlines around the world as he becomes the first Brazilian ever to play in the World Series. Lining up for the Kansas City Royals, it's been a double celebration for the São Paolo born player as his team brought home the trophy, defeating the New York Mets four games to one.

2 This has to be the weirdest job around, but it really happens. Families are paid to live in empty homes. The family moves in and lives in the house as normal, but they have to keep it clean. It turns out that house buyers are more inclined to buy a property if it feels like a home, so companies pay people to live in them. However, whenever a potential buyer comes around, the family has to be out. Worst of all, when someone buys the house, the family has to leave and find another empty house to call home.

3 It's the world's biggest burger and it's made right here in Southgate Michigan. Yes, we are home to Mallie's Sports Bar and Grill, where they make the largest burger in the world. We ordered one to check it out, but be warned: the burger weighs around 150 kilos and you have to order it 72 hours in advance. Don't use the drive-thru because you'll never get it in your car.

4 Russia's legendary Bolshoi Ballet has toured the United States many times, but this year the company has announced its first ever visit to Canada. Dance fans will be able to see *Swan Lake* in Toronto, followed by five performances of *Don Quixote* in Ottawa. It promises to be a once-in-a lifetime opportunity for Canadians to see the world's premier dance company locally.

5 Professor Kieran Mullen of Oklahoma University became so tired of his students failing to pay attention in class that he decided to take drastic action. Taking a laptop computer, he placed it in liquid nitrogen. At that point, the computer was still OK. The physics professor proceeded to drop the machine on the floor where it broke into hundreds of pieces. The students were stunned, but it was a hoax – Mullen had planted a broken laptop at the front of the class to use in his "experiment".

48 *page 58 exercises A and B*

K = Keith Woods, J = Jenna Doyle

K: Hello, I'm Keith Woods.

J: And I'm Jenna Doyle. Today on the podcast, we discuss how a little bit of pessimism can actually be good for you. Keith, would you like to start off?

K: Sure. We'd all love to look on the bright side and think positively about our lives. On the other hand, we view pessimism as bad, a destructive pattern of behavior. Actually, it's turns out it's good to have a bit of both.

J: Absolutely, especially when we're talking about money. It can be a financial risk to be an optimist. Believing that things will always get better encourages people to borrow. Optimists always believe they'll be able to pay it back, which is not always the case.

K: No. It's not always wise to hope for the best.

J: There are also studies that suggest that pessimistic people are more effective in the workplace.

K: Which is strange, because you have to be positive and smiley on job interviews.

J: Interviews are one thing, but real work is another. Because pessimists can predict many different problems in the future, they make better plans than optimists. Hoping that nothing bad will happen in the future is just wishful thinking.

K: True. Now one thing that surprised me is that pessimism also has some health advantages.

J: Is that really true?

K: It seems so. German doctors discovered that pessimists are 10% more likely to have better health in the future than optimists.

J: Why?

K: It's possibly because pessimists panic about health problems and seek medical attention early on. When it comes to your health, the "no news is good news" strategy is not always the best. Optimists sometimes ignore a medical problem until it's too late to solve it.

J: I see.

K: Being optimistic can be dangerous to your health in other ways. Optimists don't believe that bad things will happen to them, so they don't take basic safety precautions like wearing a helmet when riding a bike. More people are seriously injured in bike accidents because they don't have appropriate protection. Better safe than sorry.

J: So, next time someone complains that being a pessimist is "toxic", remember there are benefits to looking on the bad side of life.

Answer key

Unit 7

7.1

A 1 regarded 2 rose 3 released 4 came 5 high-profile 6 took
B 1 had 2 get 3 of 4 got 5 on 6 into
C Students' own answers

7.2

A 1 h 2 c 3 a 4 d 5 f 6 b
B 1 ~~so that~~ 2 ~~Because of~~ 3 ~~due to~~ 4 ~~since~~ 5 ~~in order to~~ 6 ~~As~~
C 1 ~~so~~ because 2 in order **to** beat 3 correct 4 ~~for~~ to 5 ~~So that~~ Because / As

7.3

A 1 F 2 T
B 1 e 2 c 3 b 4 a 5 d
C 1 profit 2 dud 3 guaranteed 4 melted 5 overseas
D 1 caught on 2 lacked 3 didn't live up to 4 backfired 5 failed to

7.4

A 1 d 2 a 3 b 4 c
B 1 F 2 F 3 F 4 T 5 T 6 T 7 T 8 F
C 1 ~~students~~ student 2 ~~was~~ were 3 ~~others~~ other 4 ~~other~~ another 5 ~~other~~ others 6 ~~other~~ 7 correct 8 ~~others~~ other

7.5

A 1 incredibly 2 occasionally 3 surprisingly 4 easily 5 disappointingly 6 hugely 7 consistently 8 cleverly 9 absolutely 10 firmly
B 1 C 2 D 3 not answered 4 B 5 E 6 A
C Students' own answers
D 1 Adele's in the quiz and these lines are from one of her songs. 2 It's a line from *Party in the USA*, Miley's first worldwide hit. 3 The word *rebel* is both a noun and a verb, in which the stress changes. 4 analysing pictures 5 the adverb modifying the verb: *seeing clearly*
E Students' own answers

Unit 8

8.1

A 1 I'm terrified of flying. 2 Prawns freak me out. 3 Unlike many people, snakes don't bother me. 4 I don't mind dogs at all. 5 I avoid giving presentations on my job. 6 Spiders make me a bit uneasy.
B 1 heart 2 passed 3 tears 4 sweat 5 stomach 6 dizzy 7 breathe
C Students' own answers

8.2

A 1 M 2 L 3 L 4 M 5 L 6 M
B 1 ~~unpleasant~~ difficult 2 ~~worked~~ lived 3 ~~boat~~ helicopter 4 ~~No one~~ Everyone 5 ~~golden~~ white 6 ~~month~~ year 7 ~~company~~ parents 8 ~~terrifying~~ amazing
C 1 couldn't 2 was able to 3 could / were able to 4 was able to 5 couldn't / weren't able to
D Students' own answers

8.3

A 1 cope with 2 spread 3 carried out 4 boosting 5 spread 6 undergoing
B A 3 B 4 C 1 D 6 E 2
C 1 popularity 2 confidence 3 promise 4 changes 5 lies 6 demands Gray adjective: afraid

8.4

A 1 d 2 c 3 a 4 e
B 1 can't / aren't allowed to 2 ✓ 3 ✓ 4 can't / aren't allowed to 5 shouldn't 6 are allowed to park
C 1 'd better 2 don't have to 3 aren't supposed to 4 ought to 5 're allowed to
D Students' own answers

8.5

A 1, 2, 3, 5, 6 and 7
B 1 mean 2 For starters 3 so to speak 4 That said 5 Trust 6 Other than that 7 Needless to say 8 Thank goodness
C talking about your fears can help you cope, breathing exercises, do some exercise, don't drink caffeinated drinks, get plenty of rest Students' own answers
D 1 being paralyzed by fear 2 the grammar: using *couldn't* to express inability in the past 3 living surrounded by fear and fear-mongering 4 the grammar: *supposed to* 5 dealing with and getting over problems
E Students' own answers

Unit 9

9.1

A 1 mingle 2 keep quiet 3 small talk 4 reveal 5 thinking out loud
B 1 We're in the process of thinking it over. 2 I showed the invitation to him by mistake. 3 Yeah, we sent them a present last week. 4 My mom thought it up. 5 I'll send them an email right away. 6 The caterers prepared the food absolutely beautifully.
C Students' own answers

9.2

A Students' own answers
B A 3 B 6 C 1 D 4 E 2 F 5
C 1 that 2 it 3 it 4 which 5 where 6 it
D Students' own answers

9.3

A 1
B 1 C 2 E 3 A 4 F 5 B 6 D
C 1 value 2 outlook 3 less 4 tolerant 5 under 6 to 7 aware
D Students' own answers

9.4

A 1 e 2 c 3 b 4 d 5 a
B ~~an apartment~~ a house, ~~robbery~~ burglary, ~~on a sofa~~ on a bed, ~~his brother~~ the burglar, ~~name~~ address, ~~lost~~ stolen, ~~messages~~ fingerprints, ~~four~~ five
C 1 ~~who was~~ 2 ~~who are~~ 3 ~~who was~~ 4 ~~who requires~~ requiring 5 ~~which are~~ 6 ~~that has been~~ 7 ~~arrive~~ arriving
D 1 arrest 2 suspect 3 deny 4 nod 5 comment 6 allow

9.5

A 1 as 2 Unlike 3 in order to 4 despite 5 Due to 6 so that 7 While 8 because 9 Although
B 1 T 2 F 3 F 4 F 5 T
C 1 ~~Not like~~ Unlike 2 ~~have~~ having 3 ~~studying~~ study 4 ~~what~~ that 5 ~~it was~~ the 6 because ~~of~~
D 1 needing to spend time alone, on our own 2 rudeness 3 different generations 4 catching people who lie 5 anti-consumerism; money isn't everything
E Students' own answers

Unit 10

10.1

A 1 looking forward to 2 got through 3 get away 4 dawned on 5 end up 6 mixed up
B 1 ~~go~~ going 2 dawned **on** me 3 got through it 4 correct 5 mixing us up
C 1 doctor 2 Japan 3 France 4 (Japanese) man / passenger 5 two free first-class 6 anywhere
D 1 F 2 F 3 F 4 T 5 T 6 F
E Students' own answers

10.2

A 1 mix-up 2 rip-off 3 breakdown 4 login 5 checkout
B 1 they are 2 it takes 3 to know 4 whether 5 it is open 6 I get
C 1 I'd like to know whether summer in your country is very hot. / summer is very hot in your country.
2 Could you tell me what time most stores open in your capital city?
3 Do you happen to know the name of a good restaurant near your home?
D Students' own answers

10.3

A clothes, meals, the cost of living, useful phrases, people's homes, the character of the people
B 1 F 2 T 3 F 4 F 5 T 6 F
C 1 F 2 L 3 L 4 F 5 L 6 F
D Students' own answers

10.4

A 1 hustle and bustle 2 homesick 3 overwhelming 4 culture clash 5 let alone 6 barely
B 1 was 2 I'm 3 gotten 4 are already 5 get 6 I'm 7 cannot get
C 1 slowly **getting** used 2 ~~got~~ get 3 correct 4 ~~be~~ get 5 ~~use~~ used 6 ~~get~~ am

10.5

A 1 blew 2 set 3 stunning 4 gorgeous 5 awe-inspiring 6 take 7 beyond
B a 3 b 5 c 1 d 6 e 4 f 2
C Students' own answers
D 1 traveling 2 the grammar: indirect questions 3 going home, making a home somewhere 4 the grammar: *be used to* 5 a report on a city
E Students' own answers

Unit 11

11.1

A 1 Sports 2 Property 3 Eating out 4 Arts 5 Education
B 1 ~~Argentinian~~ Brazilian, ~~lost~~ won 2 ~~don't~~ have to clean, must ~~always~~ **never** be at home 3 ~~Northgate~~ Southgate, ~~the day~~ 72 hours 4 ~~are frequent visitors~~ have never previously visited, ~~*Nutcracker*~~ *Swan Lake* 5 ~~oxygen~~ nitrogen, ~~two pieces~~ hundreds of pieces
C 1 biased 2 behind-the-scenes 3 an accurate source 4 keep up with 5 caught my eye 6 skip
D Students' own answers

11.2

A 1 lost 2 freaked 3 cool 4 calm 5 together
B 1 Rodrigo said there were some strangers in our apartment.
2 Rodrigo said no flights had been able to leave that day because of the volcano.
3 The mother said they had booked the apartment online.
4 The father said they could always stay at a hotel.
5 Rodrigo said he'd never forgive me for that.
6 I told Rodrigo I was really, really sorry.
C 1 Rodrigo asked the family what they were doing there.
2 Rodrigo asked when I was coming back.
3 The mother asked whether there had been a mistake.
4 We asked the family where they would go.

11.3

A 1 C 2 D 3 A 4 E 5 B
B 1 NI 2 T 3 F 4 F 5 T 6 F
C 1 d 2 c 3 b 4 f 5 e 6 a

11.4

A 1 didn't tell a soul 2 My lips are sealed. 3 spread it around 4 have my word 5 keep it to yourself 6 Me and my big mouth. 7 between you and me 8 never guess
B 1 urged me **to** do 2 ~~no~~ not 3 **to** help me 4 me **to** go to 5 ~~throwing~~ to throw 6 correct 7 refused **to** refund 8 ~~to~~ change
C 1 to repeat 2 not to tell 3 to join 4 to play 5 take part 6 to hear

11.5

A 1, 3, 4 and 5
B 1 regard 2 belief 3 matters 4 reality 5 call
C Students' own answers
D 1 a news story 2 the grammar: a reported statement 3 The Rebecca Black song from ex 7A in the lesson 4 the grammar: reporting what people say 5 fame and dealing with being famous
E Students' own answers

Unit 12

12.1

A 1 A 2 D 3 A 4 D 5 A
B 1 behavior 2 borrow 3 job interviews 4 plans 5 German 6 ignore 7 safety 8 toxic / bad
C 1 dream 2 good 3 wishful 4 safe 5 best 6 bright

12.2

A 1 be making 2 have completely finished 3 have already recognized 4 work 5 sit 6 will need 7 will be working 8 continue 9 be using 10 is going to save
B 1 We'll have finished our project by March 4th.
2 The population is bound to keep growing.
3 This time tomorrow, we'll be sitting on a beach in Acapulco.
4 Everyone will have left before/by midnight, I promise you.
5 In 2050, people are going to be living on the surface of Mars.
6 Barcelona FC is likely to win the league next year.
C 1 by Shakespeare 2 made by 3 by taxi, by midnight 4 by 10%, by even more

12.3

A 1 north-western Russia 2 –71 Centigrade 3 the water that doesn't freeze 4 when the temperature falls below –50 Centigrade 5 two days
B 2, 3 and 5
C 1 have, doubts 2 pulled, off 3 figure out 4 have, clue 5 pose, threat

12.4

A 1 It always leaves, it comes back 2 I'll watch 3 I'll help 4 it's going to rain 5 I'm not doing 6 will win
B 1 are we meeting / are we going to meet 2 're coming / 're going to come 3 'm going to write 4 's bringing / 's going to bring 5 'll call 6 'm going to stay / 'm staying 7 'll come 8 'll go 9 'll feel
C 1 ~~will arrive~~ arrives 2 ~~I'll leave~~ I leave 3 correct 4 ~~will meet~~ meet 5 ~~tell~~ will tell 6 ~~I'll get paid~~ I get
D Students' own answers

12.5

A 1 Hopefully 2 finally 3 definitely 4 certainly 5 officially 6 inevitably 7 eventually 8 probably
B 1 when the email was written 2 use it as an opportunity to travel 3 English is important for your career 4 further practice after the course 5 look on the bright side
C Students' own answers
D 1 the problems of being an optimist 2 what will and won't disappear in the future 3 the grammar: *bound to* 4 trying to make an excuse, but not doing it very well 5 imagining the future
E Students' own answers

Phrasal verb list

Phrasal verbs are verbs with two or three words: main verb + particle (either a preposition or an adverb). The definitions given below are some of those introduced in iDentities. For a full list, visit www.richmondidentites.com

Transitive phrasal verbs have a direct object; some are separable, others inseparable

Phrasal verb	Meaning
A	
ask someone **over**	invite someone
B	
block something **out**	prevent from passing through
blow something **out**	extinguish (a candle)
bring something **about**	cause to happen
bring something **out**	introduce a new product
bring someone **up**	raise (a child)
bring something **up**	bring to someone's attention
C	
call someone **in**	ask for someone's presence
call something **off**	cancel
carry something **out**	conduct an experiment / plan
cash in on something	profit
catch up on something	get recent information
charge something **up**	charge with electricity
check someone / something **out**	examine closely
check up on someone	make sure a person is OK
cheer someone **up**	make happier
clear something **up**	clarify
come away with something	learn something useful
come down to something	be the most important point
come down with something	get an illness
come up with something	invent
count on someone / something	depend on
cut someone **off**	interrupt someone
cut something **off**	remove; stop the supply of
cut something **out**	remove; stop doing an action
D	
do something **over**	do again
draw something **together**	unite
dream something **up**	invent
drop someone / something **off**	take someplace
drop out of something	quit
E	
end up with something	have an unexpected result
F	
face up to something	accept something unpleasant
fall back on something	use an old idea
fall for someone	feel romantic love
fall for something	be tricked into believing
figure someone / something **out**	understand with thought
fill someone **in**	explain
find something **out**	learn information
follow something **through**	complete
G	
get something **across**	help someone understand
get around to something	finally do something
get away with something	avoid the consequences
get off something	leave (a bus, train, plane)
get on something	board (a bus, train, plane)
get out of something	leave (a car); avoid doing something
get to someone	upset someone
get to something	reach
get together with someone	meet

Phrasal verb	Meaning
give something **back**	return quit
give something **up**	stop hoping for change / trying to make something happen
give up on someone / something	agree
go along with something	stop doing (over time, as one becomes an adult)
grow out of something	
H	
hand something **in**	submit
hand something **out**	distribute
help someone **out**	assist
K	
keep someone or something **away**	cause to stay at a distance
keep something **on**	not remove (clothing / jewelry)
keep someone or something **out**	prevent from entering
keep up with someone	stay in touch
L	
lay someone **off**	fire for economic reasons
lay something **out**	arrange
leave something **on**	not turn off (a light or appliance); not remove (clothing or jewelry)
leave something **out**	not include, omit
let someone **down**	disappoint
let someone **off**	allow to leave (a bus, train); not punish
light something **up**	illuminate
look after someone / something	take care of
look down on someone	think one is better, disparage
look into something	research
look out for someone	watch, protect
look someone / something **up**	try to find
look up to someone	admire, respect
M	
make something **up**	invent
make up for something	do something to apologize
miss out on something	lose the chance
P	
pass something **out**	distribute
pass someone / something **up**	reject, not use
pay someone **back**	repay, return money
pay someone **off**	bribe
pay something **off**	pay a debt
pick someone **up**	give someone a ride
pick something **up**	get / buy; learn something; answer the phone; get a disease
point someone / something **out**	indicate, show
put something **away**	return to its appropriate place
put something **back**	return to its original place
put someone **down**	treat with disrespect
put something **off**	delay
put something **together**	assemble, build
put something **up**	build, erect
put up with someone / something	accept without complaining
R	
run into someone	meet
run out of something	not have enough

Phrasal verb list

Phrasal verb	Meaning
S	
see something **through**	complete
send something **back**	return
send something **out**	mail
set something **up**	establish; prepare for use
settle on something	choose after consideration
show someone / something **off**	display the best qualities
shut something **off**	stop (a machine, light, supply)
sign someone **up**	register
stand up for someone / something	support
stick with / to someone / something	not quit, persevere
straighten something **up**	make neat
switch something **on**	start, turn on (a machine, light)
T	
take something **away**	remove
take something **back**	return; accept an item; retract a statement
take something **in**	notice, remember; make a clothing item smaller
take someone **on**	hire
take something **on**	agree to a task
take someone **out**	invite and pay for someone
take something **up**	start a new activity (as a habit)
talk someone **into**	persuade
talk something **over**	discuss
tear something **down**	destroy, demolish
tear something **up**	tear into small pieces
think back on something	remember
think something **over**	consider
think something **up**	invent, think of a new idea
touch something **up**	improve with small changes
try something **on**	put on to see if it fits, is desirable (clothing, shoes)
try something **out**	use an item / do an activity to see if it's desirable
turn something **around**	turn so the front faces the back; cause to get better
turn someone / something **down**	reject
turn something **in**	submit
turn someone / something **into**	change from one type or form to another
turn someone **off**	cause to lose interest, feel negatively
turn something **out**	make, manufacture
U	
use something **up**	use completely, consume
W	
wake someone **up**	cause to stop sleeping
walk out on someone	leave a spouse / child / romantic relationship
watch out for someone	protect
wipe something **out**	remove, destroy
work something **out**	calculate mathematically; solve a problem
write something **down**	create a written record (on paper)
write something **up**	write in a finished form

Intransitive phrasal verbs

have no direct object; they are all inseparable

Phrasal verb	Meaning
A	
act up	behave inappropriately
B	
break down	stop functioning
break out	start suddenly (a war, fire, disease)
C	
catch on	become popular
check in	report arrival (at a hotel, airport)
check out	pay a bill and leave (a hotel)
cheer up	become happier
come along	go with, accompany
come back	return
come up	arise (an issue)
D	
dress up	wear more formal clothes; a costume
drop in	visit unexpectedly
drop out	quit
E	
eat out	eat in a restaurant
F	
find out	learn new information
follow through	finish, complete something
G	
get ahead	make progress, succeed
get along	have a good relationship
get by	survive
get through	finish; survive
go along	accompany; agree
go away	leave a place
go on	continue
H	
hang up	end a phone call
hold on	wait (often during a phone call)
K	
keep away	stay at a distance
keep on	continue
keep out	not enter
L	
light up	illuminate; look pleased, happy
look out	be careful
M	
make up	end an argument
miss out	lose the chance (for something good)
P	
pass out	become unconscious, faint
pay off	be worthwhile
pick up	improve
R	
run out	leave suddenly; not have enough
S	
show up	appear
sign up	register
slip up	make a mistake
stay up	not go to bed
T	
take off	leave, depart (a plane)
turn in	go to sleep
turn out	have a certain result
turn up	appear
W	
watch out	be careful